PRAISE FOR ANGELA CANNON-CROTHERS

Angela Cannon-Crothers—whose *Changing Seasons* I chose for the Cayuga Lake Books Creative Prose Award—is a nature writer in the great tradition; her personal observation and appreciation are combined with scientific knowledge. She sees and records the small, beautiful surprises of the flourishing plant and bird and animal life in the woods and fields around her home in upstate New York. She knows how skunk cabbages warm the frozen soil around their early-spring shoots, and how snails find their way; she can tell you what the different calls of birds mean, and how to distinguish the night-shine in the eyes of foxes from those of deer on a dark night. She can also teach you how to make pesto from wild garlic and dandelion leaves, and what wild flowers are most delicious in salads.

Ms. Cannon-Crothers is also aware of the deep past and uncertain future of our landscape: she rejoices in the return of the bald eagle and the saving of rare wild flowers, and mourns the destruction of fertile local farmland by pesticides.

Her focus, however, is on the pleasures of seeing and hearing and understanding the natural world, which comes alive not only in her detailed descriptions but in her charming and scientifically accurate drawings. Once you have read this book, your next walk in the woods, or even your next visit to your own back yard will be different: you will see more and be more aware of the wonders that are all around us.

Alison Lurie
Pulitzer Prize-winning novelist
Professor Emerita, Department of English, Cornell University
Judge of the Cayuga Lake Books Creative Prose Award

Inspiring...thought provoking. Wonderfully crafted by a master naturalist. A must for every naturalist's library.

Mark Holdren, author of *Thoreau & Me in The Finger Lakes*

In writing *Changing Seasons in the Finger Lakes*, Angela Cannon-Crothers has proven herself to be a true conservationist and environmentalist, as well as an astute and concerned observer of nature and all of its wonders. As an environmental educator at the Rochester Museum & Science Center's Cumming Nature Center, an environmental science instructor at Finger Lakes Community College, and as a key contributor to the natural history educational programming at the Finger Lakes Museum, the author has always impressed me with her passion for the outdoor sciences and her knowledge of such a vast array of plant and animal life forms.

In *Changing Seasons*, the reader will have the opportunity to view some of the least obscure and more obvious mysteries of nature through the author's eyes—eyes that don't miss a thing—and benefit from her seasonal observations and perceptions. Since this book is intended to stimulate the reader's outdoor awareness, it is not meant to be read just once and then put away. It is instead a book that should serve as a natural history reference—season by season.

John Adamski
President Emeritus
The Finger Lakes Museum

CHANGING SEASONS IN THE FINGER LAKES

Essays and Sketches

Angela Cannon-Crothers

Cayuga Lake Books

Cayuga Lake Books
Ithaca, NY USA

Changing Seasons in the Finger Lakes
by Angela Cannon-Crothers

Copyright © 2019 Angela Cannon-Crothers
ALL RIGHTS RESERVED

First Printing – September 2019
ISBN: 978-1-68111-323-4
Library of Congress Control Number: 2019947308

Author Photo by Sophy Parshall
Cover designed by Kim Torpey
Cover and text illustrations by Angela Cannon-Crothers

Printed in the U.S.A.

0   1   2   3   4   5

Dedicated to all my former Environmental and Soil Sciences college students (in hopes that they can save the world) and to all my barefooted, nature loving, primitive skills learning Forest School children (because the future is theirs).

TABLE OF CONTENTS

SPRING

Bloodroot

March: What Are We Waiting For?

The opening of March is tightfisted and raw. Silently, within the hard shell of tree bark, a thin layer of cambium is beginning to pulse with nutrient–laden sap. The red-winged blackbirds arrive by the second or third week of the month, along with tree sparrows. Last year (and the year before) both arrivals were two weeks earlier than I expected. It's too early to put the snow shovels away when March often gives the heaviest snows and April is not too shy to offer the same. Yet here, in the Finger Lakes of New York State, spots of red line portions of the trail; festive scarlet fairy cup are the first fungi to fruit in the earliest days spring. The two-inch vessels of the cups turn blood red as they produce their spores to drift and spread in the melting snow. It appears as if the earth must bleed before surrender.

According to my records, spotted salamanders, that have slumbered underground and under logs all winter long, will emerge to lay egg masses in vernal pools and ponds sometime between March 26th and April 9th, although in 2017 I spotted a few spotteds as early as the end of February. Arriving earlier than usual goes also for the black-throated green warbler, the yellow warbler, the rufous-sided towhee, and the phoebe (although the latter not by more than a week). Such observations of earlier spring occurrences are being noted by others as well. Citizen Science organizations collect data worldwide from a consortium of professional and amateur naturalists, biologists, birders, and weather geeks. The Cornell Lab of Ornithology has a couple programs, some of the first in the nation, as does a project known as Bud Burst out of the Chicago Botanic Garden, and iNaturalist. Such phenological recording sites on the World Wide Web connect people not just with online databases, but with our natural world as well.

Phenology is the study of seasonal occurrences. Such occurrences are the notable times when the wood frogs first quack or the spring peepers begin peeping. Such quaint records of the past help gardeners know when to plant peas. Mourning cloak butterfly enthusiasts recognize when to be peaking under eaves. The feeders of hummingbirds know when to set up their sippers, and fiddlehead foragers learn when to foray. As well, keeping track of daily temperature and precipitation is one way to try and understand the fickleness of weather. The long term tracking of such seasonal happenings aides all of us in better understanding changing climates in a warming world. Melting ice caps and glaciers are not the only signs of global warming. Migratory birds sense it. Whales swim in it. Bark beetles, adelgid and insects with crop crunching mandibles flourish in it. Trees and herbs and even soil microbes all react in one way or another to seasonal changes. Such subtle warmth has a tug on all living things.

Odoriferous skunk cabbage roars within the soil before spring has fully sprung. Skunk cabbage, aptly named for its stench, exhibits the rare quality among plants known as thermogenesis; it raises its temperature to actually melt snow and icy soil around its bud. All life creates some heat, I suppose, but theirs is so evident! Just as amazing as their heat is the fact that any one of these wetland stinkers could be hundreds of years old. Possibly a thousand years old. The skunk cabbages are our elders. Creating heat is the plant's survival strategy (earlier pollination, earlier spreading into the swamp, protection....). In March, the skunk cabbage bloom is shaped like a carnivorous pitcher plant, or the toe of the shoe of a mischievous elf, or the head of a Parasaurolophus dinosaur. If I whispered to the cabbage that we humans are creating heat too, would the cabbage nod in understanding? Would the cabbage ask if this was our survival strategy also? How would I reply?

Bluebirds come looking for nesting cavities in mid-March. Woodcocks begin "peenting" around the equinox, near March 20th. Our ancestors noted this event of near equal hours of daylight vs. night-ness with rituals and celebrations. Such a date urges us to be inspired for the season ahead, or reminds us to be more balanced, at least. We wait for the first dandelion greens to nibble, for the first shadberry blossoms spraying the hillsides with their white foamy hues, for forsythia to glow, final ski runs on corn snow, and working the soil. We watch for all the signs of a changing season with expectation and joy, but there grows a new rub in the shift.

Near March's end (so far) the wide-wing'eds come soaring back in the upper air thermals. These glorious birds with upswept wings are turkey vultures. They take on the thankless business of cleaning up carcasses from winter's toll and hit n' run road kills. From single-minded striped skunks to pavement—hopping peepers, they do not discriminate. But turkey vultures have no spring call or vocal chords at all. Their early return is the simple whisper of a warming, incessant, wind. Theirs is a silence drifting overhead, the signs we don't notice unless we look carefully. Their arrival is the reminder that we expect nature to clean up our calamities.

Is that what we are waiting for?

Searching for Sheds

Spring. The salamanders already emerged and I have even heard a woodcock peenting, but today the wind is blustery with snow.

"Maybe you should try looking over here!" My neighbor, hunting mentor and dear friend, Lou Abbondanzieri, shouts from across the fields.

I walk toward the edge of the turnip field, looking carefully for some sort of fracture of grey-white within the powder-white of light snow. "You have to slow down, look carefully," Lou adds, and then tells me to come closer his way. When I see the four tines of a large, single antler frozen to the ground, I give a little yelp. Then I laugh because I realize that Lou, of course, found the shed first and was merely guiding me to it.

Bucks shed their antlers anywhere from winter to early spring. Searching for sheds is akin to a puzzle painting where hidden figures are camouflaged within the landscape and you just have to learn to see what is actually there. There is so much we don't see, even when we are looking for it. One must learn to spot a change, like the slope of shape within a rocky field, or the scent of the shade of color different from those of the branches on the forest floor. It seems like magic to find one, but Lou knows where to look - near feeding areas, along deer trails and bedding areas. Mastery of the mystery I guess, but antlers do contain many myths. Antlers are a symbol of regeneration, spiritual authority, and survival - maybe because to find one is a sign that the buck made it through hunting season. In Celtic lore, deer where herded by fairies and antlers symbolize prosperity, growth, and spring fertility.

Male deer's hormones kick in at just over a year in age and begin to grow antler "beams" from blood-flowing pedicles on their crowns, come spring. Antlers are honeycombed, bone-like tissue covered with a velvet that supplies nutrients and minerals via nerves and blood vessels. Antlers are some of the fastest growing bones known. In a season of lush greens from rich soil, more than 200 inches of antler on a single deer can grow in about 120 days. Each set of antlers is unique to the deer which grows them. None are identical. A buck's rack represents his identity, age, genes, diet, the soil health, and stress in his environment. Antler size helps assure their genes will be passed on. But big racks only come from healthy herds.

In wintertime, when there is a drop in testosterone hormones, the pedicle at the base of the antler begins to weaken and close off. Like a tree closing off nutrients to its leaves in the fall, the antler dies and then, molts, falling to the earth. The process can take two to three weeks.

Mice, birds, squirrels, porcupines, foxes – and even bears – will peck, gnaw, chew, drill, and maw the drops because they are rich in minerals like calcium and phosphorous.

"Glassing for tines" is the expression used when one uses binoculars to search a winter field of corn or clover from the comfort of one's truck. Antlers have many uses. They can be boiled and strained for a gelatin to use in jellies, or fire—baked and ground to use as a baking powder, sawed and drilled for buttons, made into knife handles, rattling antlers, chandeliers, lamps, jewelry, toggles, coat or towel racks, toilet paper holders, dog treats, centerpieces, a cribbage board, or sold for money.

I find three more antlers (actually, Lou guides me to the match of my four—pointer and I think I find the third – a small three tined antler in the sawgrass—all on my own, but I'm not so sure). As we start heading back I see the figures of deer leaping past the thin trunks of trees beyond the field. "Look!" I tell Lou, pointing, excited I saw something before he did this time. Then I see something even more amazing—a buck still in full rack, running along with the rest.

I imagine springtime sprites are rustling up the herd, showing me a reason to come search for sheds again, later this spring. Maybe, too, they are encouraging me in my practice of this art of seeing.

The Deep Under-The-Green

The landscape is awakening.

It's easy this time of year to see the life force sweep across the land, resurfacing it with growing, living things lifted up by the warmth of the sun. The web of life bursts forth like waves to the shore with each bud and blossom. It would also be easy to mistake such a sight with the presumption that "all of creation" is only here on the surface of our rare earth; just a thin coat that serves as a shell and the only place that can support biotic activity, but is it so?

As I dig down to pull up a dandelion whose deep tap root (excellent for strengthening the liver and whose green leaves can provide the depth of my own tiny cells with important nutrients), I peer into the amazing ecosystem of microbes that help make all this upper green possible. Everything from arthropods and soil nematodes to bacteria and fungi who keep the process of decomposition and nutrient recycling moving for the rest of us are here. The intricate webs of fungi mycelium themselves can be a couple square feet in size to over thirty square miles for a single individual. Millions of unseen creatures in the soil layers are working, busy, making the contributions necessary for life on earth as we know it.

Further down—much, much further down—is a place we imagine as a dark and mineral world void of life with merely a structural sort of function. This is also wrong. Sandra Steingraber, author, ecologist, and human activist for chemical contamination, wrote in the January/February 2013 issue of *Orion Magazine* how the amazing discoveries of "deep life"—not in the oceans, but in the bedrock—extend our notions of the biosphere up to three miles below the surface. Take for instance, ancient bacteria that use hydrogen for energy and transfer electrons into the mineral rock around them that exist in deep bedrock in colonies and communities creating their own vital cycles to Earth's homeostasis. Incidentally, these bacteria are estimated to have been present on Earth for about 85% of the planet's history. Mankind? Our presence is just a mere blip of time – the last five minutes of the clock—in comparison. Even more astounding, a species of roundworm (a multicellular creature) was recently discovered over three kilometers below the earth's surface. Writes Steingraber, "Deep-life organisms are ubiquitous and almost certainly play a role in the Earth's carbon cycle. They may, in ways we do not yet understand, contribute to climate stability." It appears that the mystical Middle Earth, the deep, deep, underground being blasted and injected with untold chemical stews from hydrofracking gas extraction, is actually somebody's home; a somebody whose function and contributions to the planet as a whole isn't understood one iota yet.

Now, I'm not trying to give some Spotted Owl battle cry (not that I wouldn't) to save the roundworm, *Halicephaobus mephisto*, or to protect an ancient radioactive fixing bacteria that might come in handy for cleaning up some of our other messes, but rather to ask that we consider not just our fresh drinking water and our clean air (which by the way, turns out to also harbor amazing microscopic critters way up in the atmosphere) but the deep underground we know so little about. Soil and rock are part of an amazing geo-microbiological system that forms the foundation of a planet that just happens to be the one we live on; one that in the deepest depths of the entire universe, seems to be the only one we have that will support us.

Dandelion in hand, I pull the root up from these depths in wonder. There is some sort of life force deep down within the earth and I realize Earth really is Gaia, a living organism. I shake the dark dirt full of hundreds of miniscule microbes off the dandelion root and leaves that will nourish my own cosmos of cells, that I will wash clean with the sweet deep well water from my faucet that is still safe to drink as I take a full, deep breath and remind myself what a blessing this all is, how we should never take any of it for granted, no matter how deep, or distant, it seems.

A Paddle Through
Environmental History

The teenagers from Pittsford High School, all dressed in red and blue life jackets and paddling the aluminum canoes in a zig-zag of confusion, are louder than a construction zone. I realize our chances of seeing much wildlife out here on the Honeoye Inlet at Finger Lakes Community College's Muller Field Station are probably next to nil. But theirs is a joyful noise so I try to let it wash over me with calm assurance that despite their inexperience, nobody will end up in the drink.

I want these kids to notice the beaver scent mounds all along the channel's edges between freshly risen royal fern. I want them to look for signs of otter slides along the banks, to spot the numerous brightly feathered warblers singing from branches of maple, ash, speckled alder and highbush blueberry that inhabit this swamp ecosystem. It's hard to get them to "see." They are too busy navigating and experiencing new paddling skills for one thing, so how can they attend to the signs of nature they don't know they could be missing?

Rafted up, I asked them questions about what is visible to my eyes, for which they have no reference to discern from the environment—the caches of twigs, the chewed down alders, the piles of castor odor mud. Beaver were once nearly extirpated from New York State due to heavy trapping for their fur, especially when beaver felted top hats were all the rage until the mid-1800s. I also explain that this silver maple—ash swamp is a designated wetland, but when land conservationists, Emil and Florence Muller, had these channel waterways dug in the early 1960s, there was less protection for wetlands. Wetlands were drained for farmland or filled for dumps or residential uses, before we acknowledged their importance in flood control, groundwater recharge, and essential wildlife habitat. The Wetland Act could still use some improvements, but at least the foundation is here.

Otters too were gone from our region just thirty years ago. In 2000, a restoration effort was begun on Honeoye Lake and now, sixteen years later, sleek otters swim the shorelines looking for freshwater clams and mussels. Some even venture up the gullies into Wesley Hill Preserve, Cumming Nature Center, and further afield, expanding their range.

Two bald eagles soar at the south end of Honeoye Lake as we paddle further on. I tell the students how, when I was a child, there were no bald eagles here, or anywhere in New York, or most of the Lower 48 for that matter. When I ask them if they know what happened to the eagles, they struggle to recall what they learned in their biology class. "Something to do with industry?" one student says. "Not exactly," I say. We discuss the pesticide DDT, how its use caused bioaccumulation on up the food chain, how the eagles who ate the fish didn't die, they just could no longer reproduce due to the thinning of their egg shells from the toxin. Of course, eagles were also shot and suffered from habitat loss as well. I tell them a story about how the return of the bald eagle to New York began right here, in the Finger Lakes Region.

In American history, the beaver and the otter and the eagle were considered numerous and ordinary, with no imagined end to them. Early Europeans took them all for granted, but the world is not full of ordinary things; the world is full of beings that buzz and flutter and soar, gifted with those that unfurl and blossom and grow, as well as brethren who crawl, leap, lope and run. The world is full of miraculous life of all kinds that we are kindred to.

I begin to realize that what needs to be taught is our environmental history, not just to show what damage we humans have caused, but to give inspiration about how we can make changes to reverse damage or restore ecosystems. I want them to feel empowered that they can make a difference.

If the news we portray about our serious environmental issues only creates despair, then we have accomplished nothing. If we teach fear and intolerance, using words like invasive species which is too easy a stretch to mean other races and cultures within our own species, then we are still teaching an attitude that some life is of value, and some is not. We can no longer get back the Carolina parakeet or the passenger pigeon, and our current extinction rate is said to be greater than that of the Cretaceous–Paleogene extinction event, during the time of the dinosaurs. I believe healing the Earth arises from love and deep gratitude for all of nature, and all her gifts. I believe that we motivate one another by teaching hope based on examples of what good we have done, to give heart to the good we very much need to keep doing.

On Turtle's Back

While Sky Woman was falling to Earth the animals gathered. They were concerned about making a place for her to land upon. Turtle rose to the surface of the waters. The animals knew something else was needed on Turtle's back to sustain life for Sky Woman—soil. The soil, found at the bottom of the sea and set on Turtle's back, covered the shell like a great tide giving life to Earth so that the seeds in Sky Woman's hands, and eventually all of humankind, could live upon it.

The Haudenosaunee Creation Myth presents the importance of soil. Other cultures from around the globe have creation stories that involve a god who forms humans from clay and dirt, and then breathes life into them.

Soil holds the breath of life.

The soil at my home just outside Naples, NY, according to the U.S. Geological Survey's Web Soil Survey, is Volusia Channery Silt Loam. It's a sexy name. Loam is a perfect blend of the mineral separates of sand, silt, and clay that make up all soils on earth. These three ingredients are derived from parent rock material that has been breaking down for hundreds of millions of years. And although I know that anything labeled "loam" is desirable for gardening, when I feel the soil, and squeeze a ball of it in my hand, I can sense there is more clay than silt by the way it holds its shape and sticks to my fingers, rather than feeling slippery like silt or grainy like sand. Clayish soils hold a lot of water, requiring peat moss or organic material to help keep it from sticking together into clods. Soil clods create a condition that removes valuable air space and micro pores required for the most important part of soil—all the living things that reside within.

Soil is more than part of our living ecosystem, it's a world all its own. A single spoonful of soil may contain a billion bacteria, a million fungi, and ten thousand amoebae. On a microscopic level what you see are: bear-shaped, six-legged tardigrades cantering through water droplets filled with single celled amoeba and bacteria, tiny nematodes (nearly microscopic and worm-like) flapping about in a larger stew of giant earthworms, centipedes, terrestrial crustaceans (more commonly known as sow bugs), pseudoscorpions and mold mites roaming through mini landscapes of boulder-sized sand, silt, and smaller clay particles, all surrounded by a complex network of fungi mycelium that bridge communications between the rhizospheres of grass, herb, and tree roots extending into the dark underground.

It's a lot of wildlife to think about.

This living system helps soil provide all of the nutrients, released by microorganisms, as well as mosses and lichens that not only plants need to grow healthy, but that upper world animals – like ourselves – require in order to also be well and strong. Where does the calcium from milk come from? It comes from the soil. How do iron, potassium, and vitamins get into our food? Via the soil. It is said that the authentic taste, or terroir, of fine wine, cheese, and other foods, is directly related to the soil from whence it came.

Soil does more than provide essential nutrients and the green beauty of the world; soil also sequesters carbon - a greenhouse gas. Depending on the type of soil, the organic content, weather, and health of the soil, a good, earthy dark, dynamic and decomposing soil can hold billions of tons of CO2. Healthy soil can help with our issues of climate change.

The fragrance of soil holds the dreams of the past lives of wild strawberry flowers, the rot of deer scat and it's celebratory fungi, dung beetles and worms, as well as the essence of last summer's brilliant sunshine and the spirit of the swallows chittering and swooping over the tall grasses for flies and gnats.

Soil is also joy.

I know this because when I am with children in wooded wetlands or digging in a tilled garden, they play in it, laugh in it, and cover themselves bodily in it! Being barefoot on the ground, in the dirt, turns out to be good for our spirits and minds. And how could it not be? The joy of soil brings sweet blossoms and bitter greens, shady trees to rest beneath, and a creative source for building vessels of all kinds.

The soil placed upon Turtle's back was a gift not just for supporting life, but full of its own life as well.

Salamander eggs on windowsill

Spotted Salamander Larvae
Teachable Moments

It was the end of April. Sending my daughter's birthday party guests home each with a mason jar of pond water containing a gelatinous mass of tiny egg globules was completely unplanned. That sort of serendipity occurred because when faced with six (or was is sixteen?) 10-year-olds sugared out on birthday cake and ice cream, my first instinct usually involves convincing them to go outside! And because I know that children under the influence (of sugar) require structure, I suggested we bring a bucket and some nets and venture down to the pond in my woods.

"Did you know that the ice just came off the pond here two weeks ago?" I whisper mysteriously, trying to get their attention. "Already there are egg sacks everywhere!"

The last statement sends kids scampering like toadlets all around the edges of the pond. The children play with the viscous feel of algae covered egg sacks as they drop them into the bucket now filled with pond juice.

"This pond has small mouth bass but I don't really think these are their eggs," I tell them.

"I know!" says the one token boy in the otherwise all-girl gathering, "they're frog eggs!"

"Good guess," I say. "But I think they might be spotted salamander eggs—I've seen the adults down here other early springs in the past."

That's when we unanimously decide we should each take some home and see what they morph into. Anyone taking a mason jar with pond eggs must agree to release them later in my pond, or return them to me.

For some kids—the ones with more conventional mothers who probably give out nice party favors like bags of balloons, candy, lip gloss and trinkets from the Dollar Store—I tie raffia ribbons around the tops of the jar lids so they look a bit more formal, or at least, planned. My own eggs I put in a two quart old blue mason jar. I set them on the kitchen windowsill and am happy to have something new to look at while I do dishes.

I wait, and wait, and wait.

It's nearly two weeks before little fish-like creatures begin popping out from their protective bubbles. They are less than a ¼ inch in length with long tail fins.

"Hmmm," I tell my daughter. "Maybe they are fish hatchlings after all."

When all the eggs have hatched and the critters are residing at the bottom of the mason jar I decide to try Google Images on-line to see what small bass hatchlings look like. Searching from site to site, I discover my little hatchlings seem, well, different. I type in my original egg guess, "Spotted Salamander Larvae," and new images pop up. Could be, I think to myself, but do my little guys have branching gills like those feather projections pictured here?

My eyes aren't as good as they used to be so I run and get a hand lens, which held to the round side of the mason jar, makes for a slightly skewed view. Then I think I see them: external feather-like gills, the mark of the salamander larvae.

Intrigued, I begin to do some more research. I learn that spotted salamanders, *Ambystoma maculatum*, grow to about 7 inches and can live, amazingly, 15 or 20 years. I read that it will take another two to four months for the larvae to exchange gills for lungs and form actual legs. It won't be until late summer that they will climb out of the water and head into the woods. I wonder where they are safer—with me and my feeble attempt at amphibian raising— or in their natal pond where their likelihood of becoming a meal for a myriad of other animals, from my smallmouth bass to giant water bugs, make their chances of survival statistically heroic.

Spotted salamanders spend their adult life primarily alone and underground. They emerge in darkness with other nocturnal life to consume a diet of earthworms, sow bugs, millipedes and possibly slugs—something there is plenty of around here. I also learn that the algae that cover their egg sacks actually help provide oxygen to the larvae. It's a nice arrangement.

My woodland pond is perfect breeding grounds for spotted salamanders each April when, like phantoms, they gather to quench a seasonal calling at courtship here at this place. Realizing that forest ponds are becoming rarer and rarer helps explain the declining numbers I read about in my research. Being amphibians they are also sensitive to the toxic exposure of pesticide runoff and other pollutants, habitat loss, and the warming effects of climate change.

I decide to raise the larvae to the point where I can release them on land—at the edges of the pond—so my bass won't devour them. I'm not fooling with Mother Nature; I figure if humans are a major cause of their decline, maybe a human can help them better their chances of survival. I convince myself I am just trying to balance things out.

I get out an old fish tank and my kids and I go back to the pond to collect tiny macroinvertebrates for our carnivorous hatchlings (we don't want them eating each other). We find tiny scuds under floating leaves, a few small beetles, a leach or two, and some pond weed that may contain hundreds of scrumptious appetizers only their eyes could possibly see.

That's when I get the call. Mrs. Russell, the science teacher I love to sub for at Naples Central School, needs me to come in. Middle school students love substitute teachers (although not as much as high school students who eat them alive and chew on their bones for the rest of the day). If there's two things I know, it's that an intriguing distraction can make desk-bound kids my captives for at least for 40 minutes—and kids love living things. Granted, the now ½ inch long salamander larvae aren't as grand as say, bringing in an ocelot or alligator, but they are living things nonetheless. The salamander larvae provide a perfect opportunity to talk to the students about protecting our environment, about climate change, and pollution's effects on amphibians.

Unfortunately, these amphibians live in water. Water I have to carry in with me.

A jar with a lid is a good thing, but glass is breakable and I think, potentially dangerous, so I find a clear plastic carrier with a lid that already has air holes. First period begins well and the kids love playing who-can-identify-the-critters-in-the-tank.

"It's the thing on our lab buddy sheets!" one excited child says.

"And what is that?" I ask.

It takes a bit of time but finally one student guesses correctly – salamander larvae. That's when it happens. I'm holding the carrying tank up high by the handle and the lid comes off and the tank lands on the teacher's lab table with a "scur-plash!" Water and larvae spill across the table, on the floor, and under the desks.

The kids react wildly, trying to scoop little critters into their paws. We need water to put them back in to. "Not from the sink," I say, "it's chlorinated town water!"

One student grabs the carrying container and fills it with water from the turtle tank in the back of the room. The rest of the kids are on the floor on hands and knees, some on their bellies, gently trying to pick up little larvae that flap like little fish on their fingertips.

One of the bigger boys is painstakingly trying to get a larva from under the lab table onto his finger without hurting it. "Be gentle!" he shouts to another student, "you're going to hurt it!"

After five minutes of total chaos we think we have them all back in the tank. The kids are breathless with worry—and relief.

"Are they going to be okay?" One boy asks, brow furrowed, his knees wet.

"I think so," I tell him.

"Good." he says, back to looking like his formerly tough self.

"The poor things," one girl sighs. "Are you going to put them back in your pond?" she asks.

"Yes," I say, giving in to pleading eyes and realizing I might be more of a danger to them than the bass in my pond. "Today, right after school," I promise.

Everyone smiles.

Sadly, it no longer seems like a good moment to discuss pollution and climate dangers affecting amphibians now that I've nearly killed them myself and we're behind schedule in our class work. And I still need to get some paper towels and clean up the rest of the mess.

That afternoon I bring my mason jar of salamander larvae down to the pond. While there I find a tiny spotted salamander, skirting the edge for its own meal: a survivor. Then it hits me—maybe both events served a purpose after all. The school students were interested in the salamander larvae and in wanting to save their lives. The birthday party guests were interested in the mysteries of life's renewal. Maybe they will remember that salamanders need fresh pond water in which to grow and raise their young. I know for certain the school students will remember how responsible they felt in saving them. Maybe I'd instilled a sense of stewardship in some of them, and hopefully, I didn't sacrifice many salamanders along the way.

The Songs of Birds

The language of birds seems linguistically complete. They have chirps to call their family tribe together. *Pshh*'s to speak to their young. Alarm calls. By species they also have tweets, honks, quacks, clucks, chipping, pecking, wing-drumming, wing-whirring, squawks, buzzes, dances, tail-wagging and more. But above all they have melodies. It's May and our neo-tropical summer residents are returning in steady streams, filling the morning air with a cacophony of songs as they call in mates and set up territories without fences. I've never been very good at spotting spring warblers and migrants—at least not enough to catch their field markings clearly—so I depend on my ears.

Learning to recognize songs and calls involves some familiarity with rhythm, tone, and pitch, but it can be learned. While the phoebe is an easier one (calling its name up and down the scale) other species take a more discriminating ear. I use mnemonics to help me remember some calls: the chestnut-sided warbler serenades from the trees with a "pleased, pleased, pleased to meet you!" and the common yellowthroat calls from wetland areas around West River and Naples Creek, "witchity-witchity-witchity-witch!" Further into the woods a black-throated green warbler buzzes with a "zee-zee-zee-zwheezy" and the ovenbird (named for the ground nest it builds) scolds "teacher!teacher!teacher!" Each new day of spring seems to offer up another song, and I work on re-introducing myself to one or two at a time before it gets overwhelming! The Cornell Lab of Ornithology has a great website on bird songs at www.birds.cornell.edu.

It's early morning and walking past my pasture I hear the merry chatter of bluebirds and the synthesizer voices of bobolinks. I head down into spruce and pine woods and suddenly the canopy is full of songs. I am trying to pick out tones and melodies, trying to recognize each bird; over there is the chipping sparrow calling in a rhythm each seven seconds, followed immediately by a warbler, echoed back by the ethereal flute-like notes of a wood thrush. A crow caws with crescendo and below it all the stream rushes with steady allegro. I am in awe. If I let go of trying to identify everything and just listen, what I hear is this— a finely tuned symphony of an ecosystem in unison, one song with many parts, each lifting the other.

I wrote the poem which follows to help me remember bird song mnemonics and the habitats of the different species. It is written also as a tribute to the poet Emily Dickinson whose style of iambic meter I attempted to imitate. Almost like a bird song.

Spring Bird Song (a tribute to Emily Dickinson)

"The saddest noise, the sweetest noise,
The maddest noise that grows,—
The birds, they make it in the spring,
At night's delicious close."

-Emily Dickinson

First to appear are the Bluebirds
upon the wires here
who pitch their songs proclaiming
spring—at last, is here.

The geese have all been passing
overhead for weeks by now
The Red Tail, Sharp Shinned, and Vultures too
leave their shadows on the ground.

Then a Phoebe calls its name-song tune
and flaps its tail in wagging;
with the promise of a nest below
the hayshed's timber hanging.

A Robin cheery-o, cheery's-me
while scratching in dead leaves
as loud as any squirrel might be
below my bedroom eves.

"Pleased-pleased-pleased to meet-you!"
A warbler greets my ear
and if I search him in the limbs
I see his chestnut-sided tears.

"Sweet-sweet-sweet, I'm so sweet"
The Yellow Warbler sings
without whose song the cacophony
would bemoan a sorrowful thing.

The Orioles do hang their nest
like baskets woven well
now spring comes all-the-sooner
as science does foretell.

Finally, when flute songs play,
in the deeper woods below,
I know the Hermit Thrush returned
announcing no more snow.

There is a hut-like little home
built on the forest floor
where calls a plain brown Ovenbird
"Teacher! Teacher!" he implores.

"Zzee-zzee-zzee-zzee Zee!"
buzzes a Black Throated Green
somewhere at the gully edge
in piney forest, sight unseen.

From high up in the treetops
another winged-soul's return—
a Red Eyed Vireo whose endless banter
is like a Robin without a tune.

"Witchity-witchity, witchity-witch!"
I hear the battle cry
and wonder what makes the Yellow Throated
think he knows anything of I?

Barn Swallows bully Bluebirds for the boxes
I clean out every year
but still devour mosquitoes and bugs
and so I hold them dear.

And if *Hope is the thing with feathers*
that perches in our souls
then so are the birds who return each spring
a blessing to us all.

Wild Ginger

Of Snails and Spring Ephemerals

It seems that over the winter my garden grew weeds, rocks, and snail shells. The snail has trailed through my life like a sparkling path spiraling out from center at all major milestones in my growth. I'm fascinated by the symbolism of this native mollusk's spiral shell as a totem for our lives. The snail shell is an equiangular (or logarithmic) spiral. The form follows what is known by mathematicians as The Golden Rule; a divine design that maintains that as the form increases in breadth, it maintains its ratio. This beautiful curve, practiced by nature since the beginning of time, intrigued ancient Egyptians and Greeks as well as more modern mathematicians like Bernoulli (1654-1705), who requested that the spiral be engraved upon his tomb with the phrase, *Eadem mutata resurgo, meaning,* "I shall arise the same, though changed".

Eastern forest snails, *Anguispira alternate*, are in the same phylum as clams, oysters, and mussels, and in their own class with slugs. Characterized by waving eye-spot tentacles, mysterious spiral shells, and trails of sparkling goo, who wouldn't find them wondrous? As it turns out, there are some 115 species of land snails in New York State, most of which are native and an important part of the ecosystem. Snails' mouths contain a chitinous ribbon called a radula and are lined with rasps to shred leaves and plant debris. Snails, besides being terrific at helping prepare ground matter for decomposition, are also an important food source for birds and other wildlife.

Curious about the rasped mouth of the snail, I located a snail (quite easily) and with magnifying glass in hand, I set him upon my thumb. I don't know what makes snails so inquisitive and trusting, but it took only moments for the little beast to begin unfurling from its shell. First he stuck out one upper eye, then the next, waving them back and forth toward my own eye gazing through the hand lens. Then he stuck out two lower eyes, and seemed to use them as feelers to sense whatever form of non-terra firma he was on. Their lower eyes, it turns out, are more for sensory detection.

I recently read that Americans may want to learn how to domesticate these one-footed gastropods for protein. Simply put, you must capture the snails (doesn't sound too difficult) and contain them with clean kitchen waste clippings and daily washings for about a week or two until their poo looks like what you are feeding them. In order to continue to avoid any bad taste or possible parasites (like brain worm nematodes you wouldn't want to catch) the little snail must be thoroughly boiled. Supposedly these are good with butter and garlic. I wouldn't know.

Springtime is mating season for many animals and the snail is no exception. The snail's reproductive strategies however, are exceptional. Snails are hermaphrodites, that is, they have both male and female reproductive structures. In spring you may find a snail on a mission; eye tentacles winking and waving and full of Eros for its nearest neighbor. Upon finding one another, any two lascivious snails mate in a full front foot caress of goo. Eventually, both snails will slime trail away to lay a batch of tiny purl eggs under logs, bark, or yard debris as both the mother and father of two separate broods.

For me, snails are usually far less offensive than their cousins – the slugs. Slugs attack my lettuce, devour my first veggie sprouts, and gulp all the mushrooms I attempt to inoculate and grow around the farm. Snails are just so much easier to toss over the garden gate. Snails are friendly too and put in hand, don't mind taking a rather brave look at you.

When my children were young I used to tell them that snail trails were where the fairies had walked the night before. My daughter and I used to have a ritual at night based on the book, *I Love You As Much* by Laura Krauss Melmed. Both of us would try to think of the grandest or most outrageous examples of our love for each other. One night, when I was in an especially stressed mood and just wanted her to go to bed! my daughter said out of the blue, "I love you as much as the snail has weird eyes."

Yeah, there's nothing like the snail.

Spiraling back to the first time I visited Grimes Glen in Naples in springtime, I remember being awed by the wide array of spring ephemerals: the gems that bloom for only a few short weeks before the trees leaf out and shade the forest floor. Just a short stroll down the south side trail revealed the tiny purple stars of blue cohosh, three species of trillium (nodding, white and red or wake robin), speckled trout lily, tiny mayflower, cut-leaf toothwort, spring beauties and many more.

Both rue and wood anemone blossom here in the shale soils of the gully. Anemone are named for the Greek god Anemos and are said to have originated from Mount Olympus, though another legend says the anemone flowers were Venus's tears after she lost her love, Adonis. Delicate snowflakes of miterwort bloom now and will give way to taller white foam flowers whose Latin name *Tiarella*, comes from the Greek, "little tiara" because of the tiny yellow pistils that rise above each delicate white blossom. Both true and false Solomon seal are found now, the true having its flowers dangling all along the stalk of leaves. Yellow barren strawberry flowers are prolific, but not nearly as much as the variety of wild violets to be found. Violet flowers and leaves are wonderful to collect for teas, salves, candied flowers, and salads (just collect them on your own property as Grimes Glen is protected partially through the Finger Lakes Land Trust and managed by Ontario County Park).

Last year I was saddened to discover that a large patch of wild ginger, also known as heart leaf or birthwort, was gone from alongside the trail. Folk medicine uses the ginger-scented root as a tea for easing pains of pregnancy and as an antibiotic. The tiny purplish-brown bell-shaped flowers sometimes called "little pig's feet" or "little brown jugs." At first I was angry and thought that someone had dug up the wild ginger plants but then I discovered some insect or other had devoured them. Looking more closely, I realized that snails and slugs apparently go gaga over this plant too.

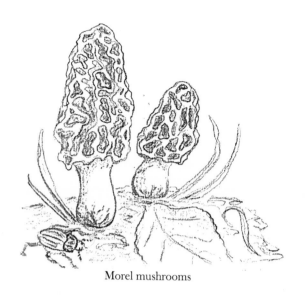

Morel mushrooms

The Forager's Way

There is something to gathering, some ancestral link between our spirits and earth that is softer and more at ease than toiling in the garden. Both have their rewards, but going gathering tunes one into the natural world at a different pace. As a forager one is hunter, but not predator. The fields and forests demand different eyes just the same, a sort of tuning in that becomes watchful and mindful; a way of being that finds gratitude in a bounty given freely for those who seek it out.

At this stage in our evolution most of us believe that the only good—or safe—food is what we purchase at the market. Or perhaps what we plant intentionally in our gardens. It's a misconception because as omnivores with an enormous palate for a variety of tastes, the fields and forests offer so much more variety, often with far more nutrient value, than with our accustomed veggies.

I started making wild pesto a few years back, and it is one of the easiest and tastiest ways to use wild greens that also makes a great conversational pot-luck dish. All that garlic mustard that takes over an entire forest opening is the main ingredient for a great pesto. Gather the leaves by the bushel and remove stems. Add a few handfuls of young dandelion leaves, small plantain leaves, wild onion or leek greens, some olive oil and grated parmesan and blend in a food processor. Adding a few sunflower seeds or other nuts adds additional flavor and texture, but isn't necessary.

Wild salads are another way to pack in extra vitamins and minerals, as well as interest and flavor, to any traditional lettuce variety. The leaves of lamb's quarters, pigweed, young plantain, young dandelion, and wild mustard are perfect choices. You can add even more beauty to any salad with the addition of edible wild flowers like violets, red clover, and wild roses—or the dandelion flowers themselves.

I once heard a shaman herbalist tell the story about our plant world being our closest allies in Nature; that the plant tribes are here to help us heal and keep us strong. The plants we most often consider weeds are probably the most important of these because not only do they offer us food and medicine, but they help enrich our soil as well. Ask any good farmer why they are letting wild mustard take over a fallow field, or planting clover, and they will tell you how important plants like these are for enriching the soil to keep it healthy.

Too often we look at what is sprouting up all over our lawns and gardens, and grimace—but the weeds in your own backyard are probably exactly what your body, mind, and spirit need most. And what we call "invasives" might be sprouting up around us because there is something in them we need to cure ourselves with or use to mend our exhausted soil. That's not to say you should just go nibbling on everything out there; find a good edibles identification book or two and take some walks with a naturalist. Always know what you are picking, if where you are picking is clean and not exposed to pollutants, and what part is edible when. Cattails, for instance, have edible flowers but only before they turn to fluff. Certain nuts need to be leached of their tannic acids. Overall, the wilds are brimming with new flavors and great nutrient value. Maybe it's time to start counting all our blessings in this Garden of Eden, and tell your friends you're going out back to gather some food.

Doing What We Do

Sometimes I have to ask myself—what am I doing? Why would anyone live this way and raise kids way out here in what amounts to a shack in the woods too far from their school or even the bus stop, with no TV, dishwasher, microwave, or typical amenities, working her tail off to raise food and have animals and piece together just enough work to barely survive? Damned if there aren't more things broken then are in repair. The wood tarps lay deflated on their pallets reminding me daily what will need to be restocked by summer's end, the horse is having issues, the hayshed roof is leaking, the garden isn't even planted yet, and I just butchered a chicken after a long exhausting day because I had to or I'd lose the meat for certain.

And why would anyone want to grow their food or plant a garden anyway? You can buy vegetables at the store, for heaven's sakes. And once you wear yourself out digging and mulching, battling herbivorous critters, hauling water and hoses, getting sunburned and bug bit and all that—success means you now get to harvest, cut, dice, boil, can, dry or freeze it all for winter! Not to mention the weeds one tries to pull out are usually higher in vitamins and minerals than many of the vegetables you planted intentionally. These hens who require twice daily care of water and food and letting in and out and the worst kind of cleaning up give us eggs—so what? Can't I just get those pallid store bought kind for far less expense?

I recently ran into a dear old friend, DJ Kitzel, at the West River where he was putting his boat in with his daughter, having driven down from the city of Rochester to do so. We got to talking about the environment and life as we usually do. As the toads began their evening trilling, he commented that he tells people he knows a place where the community is about sustainability; how some folks there raise grass-fed organic meats, others, all-natural lettuce and produce, some make natural soap, run community gardens, are artists, cheese makers, great musicians—all of it. Are we cutting edge or simply quaint, I wonder? After all, I recently heard on an NPR show that cities are the best model of sustainable development, being the intricately functional cells that they are. Out here, I have to save up gas money and make up the time it costs me just to go visit the city. So why the heck would anyone want to live so far from everything going on?

Why would anyone make their own medicines from wild crafted weeds and garden herbs and even worse, teach women who are ill and have plenty of doctors willing to prescribe them the plethora of synthetic pills we are bombarded with by the media daily, to learn to heal themselves with herbs instead? Taking a pill is so much easier. And they make one for just about anything (except what I have). So why bother? And for that matter, why would I waste my time encouraging five-year-olds that their sense of wonder and affection for dandelions is a worthy attribute when one of the teacher's parent helpers is there scoffing my every remark about the virtuous healthful qualities of dandelions? Won't these kids grow up to be just like their parents—investing huge sums of money to eradicate the yellow blossoms with dangerous toxins, too?

And why would my neighbors and herbalists, Andrea and Mathias Reisen, at Healing Spirits, in Avoca, spend all that dough on photovoltaic panels they won't be able to pay off for years when electricity already comes straight to your house from the hallowed and amazing grid? Why go broke trying to be green? Why buy organic when cheap food is, well, cheap? Why diversify your garden like some ecological system when with a monoculture crop and a few heaping sacks of pesticides you could actually sell some for a profit (maybe)?

I ask myself these, and many other questions, as I step off the porch into the light of a new day, ready to bend my aching back to the tasks again today (and how long can I keep this up?). Heading up the driveway to the garden I stop dead in my tracks: there, right on the center of the shovel handle I left stuck in the soil last night, below the turbines slicing slowly through an unseen wind, is a bluebird. Just sitting there. On my shovel handle; looking like, as e.e. cummings would say, a true blue dream of sky.

I stop. I am in the moment. This is the moment. There is no distant future when things get better, when we learn to live in right livelihood, sustainably, as if the earth mattered. We are here now.

I have a pack of seeds in one hand. I have faith in the other.

I figure this is why all of us do what we do.

SUMMER

Summer Solstice Nights

Summer Solstice just passed and now intense lushness erupts as if the great bear of earth had suddenly shook itself to wakefulness; its first yawn a sparkling of blossoms, its first stretch a brilliant green. Today the bear walks on and each thumping step spreads a new color—the deep green of dark forests, avocado skins, seaweeds. Just now I'm considering getting peacocks for the front yard. What I recently saw as the bare limbs of branches, views of the hills south, and rocky ground, is now a plethora of growth akin to some tropical forest. Summer has officially arrived to the North.

Like many, my garden was later than usual getting in this year, partly because of the very wet spring and partly because the chickens kept flying over the garden fence and devouring freshly planted seeds of zucchini, soy, and other beans before I got my dander up and clipped their wings. Right now the garden is more promise than food and the dreams of fresh peas, hot peppers, and someday—corn, keeps me weeding the rows. A neighbor told me the other day that this is the first year she's consciously decided not to grow a garden and how she can now go out on the porch at the end of the day and just enjoy doing nothing. I was shocked at first (I seem programmed for some sort of self-sufficiency, like a sort of survival instinct, I guess) but I think I get it; summer is short and lovely so why not just enjoy its mere presence without sweating to bend it to one's will and working it to the bone?

Although the season seems short at 42 degrees N latitude, the nights are long at last and there's an urge when the house has grown hot and stuffy to spend the evening outdoors where it's languid and cool. Lightening bugs are out in full magical array and they love the neglected areas of the property where the phlox and grasses are tallest, just near the border of woods. When I was a child my family would go to Grandmother Crothers's house in Elkton, Maryland, every summer. I looked forward to eating Chesapeake Bay crabs and catching jars of fireflies. Nana, as we called our grandmother, would take a used mayonnaise jar and carefully punch holes in the lid. My twin brother and I would run around the yard catching fireflies until our jar was full, our legs tired. The jar would be our nightlight and in the morning, when the blinking glow of lights were gone, the beetles were set free.

Lightening bugs, or fireflies, are *Coleoptera* (true beetles) in the family, *lampyridae*. There are thousands of species of fireflies but not all of them produce the luminescent glow made from a chemical reaction between oxygen and luciferin in special cells in their abdomen. Scientists have much to learn about this amazing light reaction that produces almost no heat. Different species of lightning bugs create different patterns of blinks to attract mates, and although there has been some research done regarding "false calls" by females to lure in males of other species for prey, most adult lightning bugs feed on nectar and pollen only.

Summer nights are fascinating to explore once you get your eyes adjusted. Humans see as well as a bear in the dark and according to David Stokes, author and naturalist, we can learn to see as well as a cat in the dark with some practice. I've led many night hikes over the years and enjoy assisting all ages in learning to feel the path with their feet, tune into their heightened sense of smell as warm, moist ground gives off scent, and listen for the sounds of nocturnal animals.

The best way to take in the night is to turn all outside lighting off and allow your eyes to adjust for 10 to 20 minutes. Our eyes have two main structures for dealing with sight: cones in the center of our eyes that allow us to see color, and rods along the outer portions of our eyes to let in light. Most nocturnal animals have more rods than cones and so see better in the night-ness they've adapted to. In order for us to see best in the dark we have to learn to use our peripheral vision and take advantage of the rods we have. The rods in animal eyes are what we often see as eye shine. By using a flashlight covered in red cellophane (I've used red construction paper pretty successfully too) you can explore more easily and not interfere with your own eye adjustment or startle animals by carrying a bright light. To our eyes with a bright light, deer eye shine is hot white, and red eye shine, close to the ground, is probably a fox or rabbit. You can even see the tiny eye shine of spiders with a flashlight while looking along the branches of shrubs and porch railings.

Evening sounds include the trills of toads and tree frogs, the chirps of crickets, the occasional yips of coyotes, and the hoots of owls. The barred owl, common here, makes a call that sounds like "who cooks for you, who cooks for you aaaaall?" Learning to imitate the call can actually bring the barred owls in close as they try to discover who is in their territory. Grey or red phased screech owls reside right in the village of Naples, NY, and make a wild whirring call that falls down the scale like notes on a flute. We are fortunate in town here to have so much forest around.

Once your eyes are adjusted to the night everything seems to give off its own shine, the world is illuminated by the stars above or just a sliver of moon. Taking time to sit back and admire the stars is nourishment for the soul, part of an ancient tradition that has provided us with rich stories and great wonder over the centuries. Native American cultures have constellation myths that, to me, seem fitting to North America. For instance, the Iroquois, or Haudenosaunee, of our region, saw the square of the Big Dipper as a Great Bear. Algonquin myth saw the stars in the Milky Way as campfires of their ancestors on the journey beyond, something I always found comforting.

Summer nights are full of mystery and magic. Let the wonder begin.

Spotting Eagles

It was a warm and sunny spring day at Hemlock Lake, one of only two undeveloped Finger Lakes in New York known as the Little Lakes and recently purchased by the state. I was working as a kayak and canoe guide for Pack Paddle Ski out of Lima, NY on a day trip touted as a paddle to see bald eagles.

After introductions and instruction on paddling, safety, and boats, I gave my little spiel on the return of the bald eagle to New York State. I had forewarned the eager guests that nature was unpredictable, and we may not spot an eagle here today. Regardless of our wildlife viewing, I would guide them by car later to a well-known eagle viewing site on the south end of Conesus Lake where we could see their nests, and hopefully, eagles.

Eagle nests are protected by law and signs posted by the conservation department warn of fines for anyone who approaches too closely. Even so, if a majestic bird with up to a 6 foot wingspan could not be seen in flight, their nests, which are typically the size of a small Volkswagen Bug, are pretty conspicuous even from a long way off. Plus, eagles usually have more than one pterodactyl sized nest in their territory, just in case they need a back-up.

I got my group into their kayaks and guided them across the lower end of the lake toward the winding creek inlet where we could explore. I was desperately watching and coaching my paddlers while I searched the sky for eagles. Oh please, I pleaded to the Forces-That-Be, let us see an eagle so the group feels like they got their money's worth. It was right about then that everything happened at once.

Not one, but two bald eagles had been perched in the poplar trees along shore all along. They flew out right at us with wide wings and cross faces. Maybe it was the power of their flight, or just coincidence, but right then a gust of wind tore over us, took off my bright green straw cowboy hat, and dropped it into the water.

"The eagles!" I shouted and then, "my hat!"

Nearly panicked and reaching over to grab my hat from the water, I noticed the largest snapping turtle I had ever seen swimming right underneath my kayak in the shallow weeds. "A sna-sna-snapping turtle!" I practically screamed. Heavens to Betsy, all I needed now was for one of my guests to dump their boat in all the excitement. I checked, one boat stuck in the shallows, everyone upright.

"That way!" I pointed, "there they go!"

Fifteen minutes into the guided Bald Eagle Paddle and we already spotted a pair.

To see an eagle is like getting an unexpected gift. It still exalts all the bragging rights of winning an I-saw-it trophy. There are now some 112 nesting pairs of bald eagles in New York State. This number is up from just one nesting pair in New York in 1960, about the time they were put on the Endangered Species List. Thanks to DEC wildlife department hacking (placing eaglets or eggs in nests) efforts over the past twenty years, eagle site locations in not only New York, but all over the country, are packed with the camouflaged eagle watchers in binoculars and camera-scopes. With each spotting of the soaring majesty of the eagle we have reason to feel glad. That doesn't mean there aren't other threats to their success. They must still contend with logging and habitat loss as well as basic issues of survival. The bald eagle has become as much a signpost of hope that many of our human-induced environmental issues can be remedied, as it is a symbol of this country. Maybe Emily Dickenson was right when she said, "Hope is the thing with feathers."

Soil and Summer Rose

You'd think after years of gardening one would have the concept that a vibrant, abundant garden requires rich soil, or else plenty of compost. Somehow I seem to have taken my garden soil for granted, and the vegetables are suffering.

My friend, Deb Denome, owner of Shimmering Light Farm in Canandaigua, just returned from the renowned sacred landscape of Findhorn, Scotland. What was once a sandy shoreline campground became world-famous for its amazing gardens. It is said the results came from listening to the land. Maybe it really was fairies, or angels, or the earth itself that told the founders of Findhorn how to create such vibrant soil – adding aged garbage (compost), seaweeds, manure and blessings to the land. Maybe it was zillions of little microbes begging for a home. Whatever it was, the actions of a handful of individuals created some of the most noted gardens in the world out of earth devoid of much promise for growing food. Maybe the message is that *listening* to the land (learning the physical, chemical and biological make-up of the soil, it's texture, and it's structure, as well as the landscape) means knowing what actions to take, and what actions not to.

Across the road from my property the farmers recently sprayed herbicide across acres of land. Within days all the clover and grasses turned yellow and died. Then the land was plowed. For almost two weeks all you could see was pale, brown soil out to the horizon, looking lifeless and barren despite the surrounding early summer landscapes of trees bushing out in vivid greens and deep hues, flowers bursting forth on the roadsides and birds nesting. The field became lifeless despite the fecundity all around.

Because everything was killed off, many of the microbes, nematodes, and fungi necessary for enriching the soil must have been done in as well. Now the field would require more work; fertilizers for one, and because of microbial imbalances, fungicides and pesticides due to the weakened health of the land.

I know the farmer has his own debts to pay, a family to feed, and a business to run. He's probably only doing the best he can the best way he knows how. But I can't help but wonder how my non-monoculture farming friends are making out? And I can't help but wonder if all that effort and such expensive chemicals are really the best course of action? I wonder—what would nature do?

On the other end of the spectrum, biodynamic gardening requires a certain amount of prayerful intentions, balancing spiritual and cosmic practices with physical requirements necessary for growing vegetables. Right now the valerian is in bloom, and these heady scented blossoms, for instance, are harvested and put into a tea that is eventually added to the compost pile, usually with a cow horn packed with manure. I don't claim to understand all that is involved in biodynamics. But it's a process some swear by. Regardless of one's practice, compost is really what it's all about - valerian tea and cow horns or not. Simply by layering grass clippings, kitchen waste, weeded greens, and some manure, we can not only create rich, living soil, but save on garbage waste destined for landfills Once we begin to develop compost we acknowledge the valuable cycles of decomposition, of reuse, and the beneficial organisms we take for granted.

In good compost all those microorganisms and bacteria actually help fight off bad bacteria and diseases, like the idea that if you use hand sanitizer all the time you are actually killing off the good bacteria (the bacterial white knights that help protect you) as well as the bad. To make a simple compost tea, fill a bucket ¼ full of compost and pour in water. Many people suggest using a fish tank bubbler or other aerator to keep respiration in balance so microbes don't deplete the oxygen, but others find that soaking the compost for a day or two and using the tea for watering works fine as is.

Obviously, it takes a long, long, time to make soil: 200 to 2,000 years to be exact. And since dirt makes our lunch, as the saying goes, having nutrient rich, healthy soil is what will produce nutrient rich, healthy foods.

The scent of wild white roses filling the air is intoxicating. The moon waltzes across the night sky and fireflies blink in patterns as full of mischief and chaos as the blooming world around.

I've been collecting wild roses both for work at Herb Haven and for home, making distilled rosewater and infused witch hazel, and for myself—a wild rose-scented brandy I can hopefully save long enough to enjoy on a cold winter day next winter. Most significantly,

I recently acquired the most beautiful yellow tipped pink rose. I am certain I've fallen in love with it.

Distilling flower essences is not so tricky and can be done right on the stove using a simple, old fashioned, canning pot distiller method. There are other blossoms you can collect the essences of, and other ways to do so. Some herbalists collect flower essences more purely, simply by placing a bowl of spring water under the inflorescence, gently dipping the flower head into the water and meditating on the special gifts the plant has to offer. Some believe that such flower essences can help heal issues of the heart, mind, and soul, as well as the body.

My daughter has been very sick and we did use some flower essences in a balm. One warm sunny afternoon I got her down to the pond for a dinner picnic to get her out of the house and into some fresh air, thinking that the best cure of all. Sitting on the dock we watched the small-mouthed bass acting crazily. As we watched more closely we began to see what was going on – literally zillions of tiny bass fry had hatched and were schooling about in like-minded clouds of intention. One of the smaller grown bass was swimming back and forth in front of the tiny fish, both trying to keep them herded near the shore and as it became apparent—to protect them from the other bass. Although this fish was much smaller than the other fish nearby, the father (I assume as the males of bass protect their hatched fry) was going after them with great ferocity, causing big splashes and lunges in what appeared to be a never-ending and exhausting mission to protect the young. I've read that bass parents, even father fish guarding their young, sometimes end up eating them, themselves. Nature can be cruel. Life is precarious.

I heard a nest of blue jays squawking while out walking but search as I could, I couldn't find the nest. Eventually I did—just a foot or two away hidden in the spruce boughs. By then the nest was being overseen by the mother jay, now frozen still, her hungry nestlings suddenly completely quiet. I wondered what she said, and in what language was she totally able to shush those noisy little birds?

That nature has such a formidable force as parenthood is well known and respected. We often compare a human mother's protectiveness to that of a bear; it is such a powerful analogy. We make metaphors about human characteristics with our relatives in the animal world, but it's considered inappropriate to do it the other way around.

Often we're told we shouldn't anthropomorphize animals or give plants a persona. I say, why not? Why do we think we are the only ones who love, the only ones on the planet with intelligence, families and jobs; the only ones with concerns for our young or the next generation? And vice-versa: why do we think it is only animals that run on instinct? I don't know about you, but sometimes instinct can be pretty powerful. And if we have instinct, why wouldn't our relatives in the living world have intellect and emotions as well?

When I feel an instinctive sense of discovery with a flower— that sense of connectedness to nature, or even rarely a déjà vu sort of experience with the world as a whole, I cannot help but wonder if all of us—the tiny fish in my pond, the birds in their nest, the healing properties of flower essences, and even the moon—aren't all in this together?

Try entertaining the idea that the breath produced by roses is some sort of language beckoning not just insects, but calling us out into the lush summer night. Their scent is luring us into recognizing some ancient language within our mind, buried deep within our cells we no longer remember but somehow, instinctively, recall.

So I except that I am in love with a rose; prickly and seasonable as any relationship can be.

Where The Wildlife Are

The creek was turbid with phytoplankton and swollen as if risen on yeast. We were paddling Honeoye Inlet, GPS in hand, searching for wildlife trip cameras that had been up for a few weeks this rainy summer. We wondered if any of the cameras might have ended up under water. "Look, right there," said Sasha Ewing, a wildlife technician at Finger Lakes Community College. We located the first camouflaged camera cache tied to a tree just barely above the water line. Back home we uploaded the disks on my computer, excited to see if they had actually caught any wildlife images or would reveal assorted shots triggered by branches swaying in the wind.

In just one small hummock of creek side land appeared: a few shots of a raccoon followed by the perfect pose of a red fox, a Pileated Woodpecker flew in, raccoons again, then a deer. From behind the trees a black bear materialized in a series of approaching images until its mug practically filled the camera lens. Then: a family of geese and their goslings visited over several consecutive dusks, numerous shots of the painted Mohawk of a wood duck, two raccoons in a mating repose, and shots of otters over several days. What the photos revealed were a plethora of activity and visitations from just one small, five foot diameter area. It was amazing how much the cameras caught, but what made the biggest impression on me was just how much wildlife are actually around us going about their business of finding food, raising families, and traveling from place to place. Clearly, there's a lot going on out there.

I was driving home quite late the other night, well, more like speeding along the dark highways with nothing more than getting there, and to bed, on my mind, when from the center line a red fox, kit in its chaw, sprinted so quickly in front of my vehicle she tossed her young off the road, and leapt in a flash-forward tumble into the grasses there. I had had no time to react but, thankfully, had not hit the fox. I vowed to slow down, keep my eyes peeled for animals. Drive like I cared about others. I saw two possums. Everywhere else there were deer crossing or shining their eyes from the roadside. Almost home, I spotted a large doe standing along the road's shoulder. Below her was a lumpy form along the white line of the road. I pulled over and got out. The doe moved slowly into the wooded edge. There was her speckled fawn, probably dead for quite a while as he was a bit bloated and beginning to smell. I spoke out loud to the deer, telling her how sorry I was for the loss of her fawn by some other passerby, earlier. I pulled her baby down the bank, much further from the roadside, making it safer for the mourning mother. I admit it, I cried.

The fact is this—we are not alone. The Little Lakes Region, and all of The Finger Lakes, are teaming with animal brethren who share this lush landscape with us. This is their home too, and they are part of what makes this area so special. I wonder how long it has been since we first developed such apathy regarding the dead along our roadsides. When did we give up on the feeling of horror and shame in such senseless deaths? Maybe it was with the invention of fast moving transportation. Slowing down is helpful. Being aware of our surroundings, probably even more so. But in some areas of the country (Florida in particular) highway departments are building wildlife culverts, underpasses, and greenway overpasses, connecting habitats and mitigating barriers to wildlife movement for amphibians, fish, and mammals. Like the images from Mueller Field Station Sasha and I were collecting, I've seen trigger camera photos from these safety corridors and the animals really do use them. It's like having faith that if you build it, they will come. Imagine our roadway trespasses with such safe routes for animals, how humane we humans could become.

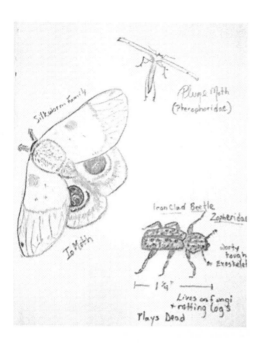

The Art of Deception

"Who is the master of disguises?" asks the little green nymph covered in its own spittle of froth. But no one answers. The nearby Geometrid caterpillar imitating a twig doesn't talk. Neither does the flower crab spider who has been awaiting unwitting prey for days on the yellow petal of a larger corollary, feeling that having to find another flower, and having to change his color again, might take too much effort.

Nature is the expert at the art of deception. A white twig is on my window and when I touch it...the twig flitters off. In the meadow I find foam between the goldenrod leaves. On further investigation, the green nymph of the spittlebug is hiding inside. There are insects that imitate other animals, parts of plants, or even–spittle. The idea behind these simulations can be for both defense against predation and deception in order to gain prey. Such adaptations of mimicry in physical form, and behavior, display the amazing evolution of natural selection.

The buff-tip moth is so convincingly a look-a-like for the birch twigs where she lays her eggs, that one would never notice her. She is the color of silvery birch, with a head that looks like the broken end of a birch twig and tail tips of a similar, freshly snapped twig color. One minute there is a twig, the next moment she takes wing and is gone. The fooled stand grappling with such unexpected reality. The critter escapes. If it's me watching a twig turn into a plume moth and fly away, I giggle in surprise. Maybe the world has a sense of humor?

How many thousands of years, I wonder, does it take to evolve physical characteristics to something one is not? Does a creature just lean into the tree and spend so much of their life sharing a sense of oneness with that species that over time they become, itself, a mirror image? Is it like dogs who are said to grow to look like their owners over time? Or couples, who in their elder years, also begin to resemble one another? Can I, too, lean against a tree for years and begin to resemble its crusty bark? Would my offspring become more and more tree-like if they did the same? But adaptations take time, unless you are, say, a fruit fly. Fruit flies lay about 500 eggs at a time and create a new generation each week. It only takes them about a month to take on a new trait or two.

Camouflage is one of the most notable of all avoidance and protective adaptations. So is playing dead, like the opossum does, but the famed opossum isn't the only one to imitate a corpse. Hog nose snakes do it. So do male nursery web spiders, and some insects. Most spiders don't like scavenging dead things (they prefer to kill their prey, maybe so they know the expiration date of their stored corpses). I recently showed some children at Cumming Nature Center a tough little iron clad beetle we found on a log that looked oh so deceased when I picked it up, only to wait a few minutes for it to come back to life and wiggle its six little legs in the air in my palm under the children's awed eyes.

The hawk moth, also known as sphinx moth, uses both camouflage and a shock factor threat for protection. These moths have a bark-like appearance on their powdery wings, but if camouflage doesn't work for protection, and a predator gets too close, they flash their underwings. Their underwings have markings that resemble brightly colored eyes of something that might be a larger predator than the one about to eat them. Fear of being eaten, over staying hidden, is the nuance here.

If none of these methods of deception work, one can always just imitate the predator one is trying to avoid. Some moths imitate wasps. Tropical metal mark moths of the *Brenthia* genus have evolved to mimic their top predator - the jumping spider. They do this with amazing wing color patterns that suggest the shape and eyes of the jumping spider while they, the moth, still maintain their own Lepidoptera form. From a bird's eye view, it's not so convincing, but get down level with a spider's eye view, and the illusion is more evident. Jumping spiders do not eat other jumping spiders, so being a look-alike spider from the spider's multiple eyes view is a perfect mimicry costume for the moth.

One of the most classic examples of mimicry in the Lepidoptera world is that of the monarch and the viceroy. We have all been repeatedly told that the monarch, who feeds primarily on the toxic plant juices of milkweed, is thus toxic to birds, so they won't eat them. The viceroy, it has been said, mimics the color pattern of monarchs so they will also be considered distasteful. This belief is now what is termed an old wives' tale (although I personally believe old wives are quite wise). Studies show that the viceroy is equally as toxic as the monarch. In this case of who is mimicking whom? Maybe the real question is: who chose their coat of arms first...the monarch or the viceroy?

Creek Walking

The soles of our feet have more nerve receptors per inch than almost any other part of the body. Maybe that is why going barefoot on the ground, drenching our toes in cool mud, or stepping into the cool of a running stream, is such a satiating sensory experience. As a child I walked barefoot in the creek bed near my house mesmerized for hours some days, waking the next morning to slightly bruised feet, the imprint of the rocks there still with me. Henry David Thoreau wrote, "Methinks that the moment my legs begin to move, my thoughts begin to flow." Walking in the flow of a stream on a hot August day, feet open to the experience, is as thought-provoking as one can get.

Although I love to swim in our clear Finger Lakes I often prefer the experience of creek walking under the cool or dappled shade of a riparian zone. Here there is a journey. Here there is quiet over motor boats and swimmers. Here there is life buzzing and oozing all around. On one such walk along Naples Creek where young boys where diving into "The Digger"—a dammed area of deeper water created for trout habitat—I ventured downstream toward the lake, creek-walking and exploring, and here is what I found: a kingfisher rattling, black damselflies, a water snake I mistook for a stick that quickly swam away, a cobble rock speckled with garnet that spoke to my heart, stonefly nymphs flat against an emerged rock, an abandoned nest in a mossy bank that was possibly a slate colored junco, fly fishing line tangled in an overhanging limb, swallowtail butterflies gathering minerals from a sandy edge of shore, a deer leg, a patch of teal blue water in a deeper pool, and the tracks of a mink.

Creek-walking does more than cool the body and spirit during the hot buzz and thick mindfulness of a hot summer day—it awakens the senses. Once the senses have opened like the pores of the feet, taking in the refreshment of the stream, the flow of life and another part of my mind opens; something akin to the creative force. There is a pleasurable mindfulness no longer aware of the duties of the day, but tuned into the ever changing watercourses, to fecundity, to movement and lushness. In this fertile place my mind begins to play with the geometry of rocks. I find rocks to gather into shapes that form giant dragonflies on a sandbar, or make rock people. I find water-soaked roots in shades of white to chocolate to shape into a basket, tie them together with grapevine also gathered nearby, and am ready for weaving. I find a few special stones that beg to be taken home as treasures from the day.

In a simple stroll to cool my body I have loosened the list of needs for the day and returned to the essentials of being. When walking these freshwater creeks or streams we are in flow; there are adventures and stories all around us, some as old as the ancient inland sea that left behind these layers of shale and slate with the occasional shell or leaf fossil. Other stories are found in the temporal flourish of the season; a hatching of stoneflies, the hunting of a Great Blue Heron, or the ripening of blackberries. How fortunate are we to have such a place, and time, to travel in.

Berry a Moment In Time

July shimmers like sun on water or a welcome breeze through denim-tough leaves. July begs for forgetfulness asking us to take time to slow down, to enjoy the season and the offering that full summer presents. I find one of the best ways to plunge into the gifts of July is to go foraging for wild berries. Berry-picking of any kind, be it a local U-pick farm, your own garden red raspberries or an abandoned field edge, is certain to pull anyone into the moment. Berry-picking makes summer stand still, for just awhile, giving the impression that the shortest season we have can go on indefinitely.

Gathering offers wilder fruits and more exotic flavors, but does require good identification tools like *A Peterson Guide to Wild Edibles.* The maple-shaped leaves of American black currants or prickly gooseberries make for exotic trail side snacks or serve as unusual add-ins to your favorite berry recipe. Thimbleberry is one of these rare fruits that I can only describe as having a flavor something between a tart apple and strawberry wrapped up in one. This velvety, large-leaved shrub with its wide pinkish red berries grows in shady areas often found while exploring our shale-filled gullies and creeks, making for a perfect combination of stream walking and gathering on a hot summer day. Like the raspberries, thimbleberry is in the rose family.

Other wild favorites include trees like serviceberry, or juneberry, a small tree whose delicious little berries are gaining popularity. Trees like chokecherry and black cherry are a bit more work because of their stones, and mulberry, a tree prolific with huge purplish fruits (there are white berry tree varieties) are so sweet you will find them often swarming with sugar-drunk bees and other insects. A bit of lemon or other tart fruit makes a good accompaniment to mulberry, whereas chokecherry demands plenty of sugar.

In more tannic or sandy soils, such as under oaks or near piney woods, one can find a variety of wild highbush and low blueberries and darker skinned huckleberries. In thicker soils, under wide umbrella leaves, you can pick may apples—if the raccoons haven't gotten to them yet.

When out gathering for abundance, the black caps, red raspberries, and later in the season – the blackberries – usually take the prize. The long thorny canes of brambles don't produce fruit the first year, but during their second year the cane produces a plethora of flowers of berries, and then dies. Some of my fondest summertime memories are of endless hours out in some field edge or dirt road, dressed in a wide-brimmed hat and long sleeved shirt and pants, with a pail in hand, just drifting in and out of thought while gathering fruits. Berry-picking is meditative. Time really does stop in a berry patch, summer stretches its neck a bit longer, worldly cares fall away with each earnest pluck focused on avoiding prickers, and as the chime of berries hitting the pail's bottom grow muted, one is reminded of the bounty earth gifts us, how blessed we really are, and how just being present and grateful for this moment in this season—sticky and purple stained as it might be—is truly the best use of our time in the end.

Great Horned Owl

What Glows in the Night

Night buzzes. Night blooms. Night unravels its mystery in long threads of conversations, each connected to the inner workings of the nocturnal world in an afterglow all its own.

A light show still pulses in tall grasses and forest edges here in the Finger Lakes, as if someone were sprinkling glitter everywhere. *Lampyridae* is the Latin name of a family of true beetles we know as lightning bugs or fireflies. There are thousands of species of fireflies but not all of them produce a luminescence. The blinks of bioluminescence derive from a chemical reaction between oxygen and luciferin in special cells in the beetle's abdomen. Scientists are still learning about this cold light reaction that produces almost no heat.

If you spot a lightning bug flying and flickering about in the darkness, it is probably a male. Females sit like indifferent wall flowers, observing the mating show and blinking back only if interested. Different species of lightning bugs create different patterns of blinks to attract a mate. Sometimes I try counting the beat of their flashes, trying to ascertain the mysterious rhythm they go by, but I can't quite get the beat. Then again, I'm not a firefly. And although there has been some research done regarding "false calls" by females to lure in males of other species for prey, most adult lightning bugs feed only on nectar and pollen. In the summer weeks to come, some of their hatched larvae—the glowworms—will glimmer on the ground.

There are other Kingdoms of Life on earth that produce bioluminescence; certain species of fungi also contain luciferin; species of *Armillaria, Panellus,* and *Omphalotus olearius* (known fittingly as the Jack-o-lantern mushroom) and a few others. These bluish-green lit mushrooms are referred to as Foxfire. Foxfire can be found glowing dimly or brightly on both down, rotting timbers, and upright trees. The original folkloric name stemmed from "Fairy Sparks" and "Fairy Fire" and was morphed linguistically to Foxfire, where other legends evolved.

A porch light in the darkness calls in numerous night-flying insects confused by the earthbound glow. Nocturnal insects navigate using the moon and stars as overhead guides and are still adapting to humankind's historically explosive transition to electric lights.

Slender-bodied, spritely colored green lacewings are common at night as are the softly scaled wide wings of moths. In early July you may find large 3-5 inches wide-winged visitors from the *Cecropia, Polyphemus,* and silk moth families, among them, the near luminescent green of the Luna moth. Equally large but more narrow in wing size are a variety of sphinx moths who swoop and buzz in flight; hence their other names as hawk moths and hummingbird moths. There are underwings, tussocks, and geometers—several thousand species of moths in all.

Some nectar-feeding and rolled-tongued species will seek out the tall stalks of night-blooming evening primrose and other moonlight blooms. Some summer night moths lack mouth parts and are just looking to mate and lay eggs on a favorite host tree for their voracious young to chow down leaf by leaf. Still others will be mesmerized by the light of a porch, a gas station, or highway lamp post, and dance the night there, forgetful of their purpose.

The eerie spots of eye shine via headlights or flashlight give us clues as to the wildlife that share our environment. We humans do not produce the reflective light in the back of our retina, and although there is some discrepancy amongst individuals, in general, white or bright yellow eye shine are most likely deer or raccoon and possum - depending on the height you see them at. Golden, dull yellow are coyotes or dogs. Taking out a flashlight and looking closely in the grasses and forest leaves, you can even find brilliant tiny red or green eye shine from spiders, or the slightly larger red shine from rabbits. Night's great masters of the hunt, the owls, may reveal red shine for a small screech owl, or large bright yellow with black pupils for great horned owls.

The hours of darkness are alive and lush with activity, the sounds of soft wings, croaks, cackles, hoots, buzzes, whirs, gnawing, and all the stuff of life.

Waldenesque Teens

"I can feel the forest breathing all around me; it pulses through my veins like wildfire...I see the forest as one living being; one body, one soul," writes Emily, one of several young teen girls participating in the week long Outdoor Writers and Where's Walden? summer camps I teach with Edgar Brown and Wendy Low at Writers & Book's Gell Center in Naples. Teaching this course each year is always one of the highlights of my summer, and this season I feel especially blessed to have the privilege of working with such inspiring young people and fine educators.

During our second morning I take my group to visit a replica of the Walden Cabin. Here I introduce them to Henry David Thoreau's life and words; to civil disobedience, abolitionists, and living deliberately and simply. We finish up in the timber frame treehouse nearby, discussing a piece by John Muir and write our own reflections. I only have a week with them so I am pouring out brief snippets from conservationists like Gifford Pinchot and Aldo Leopold, preservationists like John Muir, biologists like Rachel Carson and Annie Dillard, environmentalists like Edward Abby and Terry Tempest Williams, nature philosophers like Henry David Thoreau and contemporaries like Kathleen Dean Moore. I am reviewing the concepts of conservation, preservation and environmentalism through brief passages and small blips of these nature writers' entire lives.

The weather is unusually itchy, barbed, and dry right now. The heat and humidity send us to the trickle of creek to dip our feet in the spring fed water. Deer flies, sentries of summer days, adore us. At lunch we make a tempura batter and fry up milkweed blossoms that the teens tell me smell like lilacs, sweet and flowery. We spend the afternoon learning about edible and medicinal plants they record in field journals we created with Brown's help. Other days we study animal tracking and signs, the elements, poetry forms, essay and story. In one of our "Earth Teach Me" writing prompts Kezia writes: "Earth teach me to be aware of my surroundings, as the dragonfly is able to dart swiftly between the tangles of stems." We gather cattail leaves and I show them how to make cordage. They don't get the technique at first but before long their fingers are twisting the patterns of a skill that is thousands of years old, and soon we all don lovely, bright green bracelets made from cattail leaves.

"I noticed so much," writes Becca. "I feel like my eyes have been opened. So much life. So much beauty." As we head out to the Finger Lakes Trail on day four the students are only slightly surprised when we ask them to take off their shoes and socks near the start of the trail. This is a solo and silent walk and we want them to take it slow. "I'm really glad that we're walking the trail down alone," Becca writes again in her journal, "maybe, just maybe, if you are very quiet, if your breath is hushed and your feet are slow, if you wait in patience, you can lure your true self out." Another student, Clara, writes at the trailhead while she waits her turn: "the children will walk until the trees envelop them, until they grow roots and stretch towards the sky. Each child has a sort of solemnity that is quite beautiful...."

What I learn from teaching nature writing to children and teens is this: they are far more perceptive than we give them credit for, far more honest than most of us adults can be, and far more craving of a connection to, and an understanding of, the natural world than any of us realize. For me their words have a message for us all—"the tree is a haven," writes student Catherine, "it's a place to just get away and remember at the end of the day—we are part of nature too."

I never had to ask any of my teens to leave their iPods or other techno devices as home—they never brought them. One younger child in Brown's group said at our final closing that he was glad he came, that otherwise he would have been home watching TV and playing video games. Maybe our children are not all "teched out" and detached from the environment....maybe it is we adults who are the ones not giving them the opportunities to embrace the out-of-doors?

I know I will keep all the hope and musical words these children have gifted me in my heart all summer long. Despite all the logistical, familial, and financial struggles, I prepare for a long overdue return to McCarthy, Alaska, where I once worked for a summer, for my own writing workshop next week. I am thrilled to be workshopping with nature philosopher Kathleen Dean Moore, author of many books, including *Wild Comfort; The Solace of Nature*. Even still, I will try to remember that although the words of the great naturalist writers can be powerful and poetic, so too can those of our children, and other small voices.

Lake Emerald Dragonfly

Here Be Dragons

Broad-tailed Shadowdragon. Common Sanddragon. Ebony Boghaunter. Appalachian Jewelwing. Such names invoke fantasy images of dragons from fairytales or computer games. But they aren't from strange, unknown lands and they are real and all around us this time of year. *Odonates,* the insect order these species are part of, are the fast-flying predators of wet area ecosystems as adults. As immature nymphs, they are the mud bottom macroinvertebrate predators of lakes, ponds, streams, and forest seeps. *Odonates* are dragonflies and damselflies whose presence on Earth dates back nearly 300 million years. Here in our eco-region of New York State, latest species varieties, including the ones named above, are documented to include some 129 varieties, I think I can identify fewer than ten of them.

As a child I remember kids in the neighborhood running in terror from large Blue-Eyed Darner Dragonflies having been told that they bite, or worse, stitch your lips together. (There is a Swedish legend that says that dragonflies chase bad souls and liars to stitch their eyes, mouths, and ears closed, not that anybody I recall in my mostly Italian community was Swedish). I learned later that dragonflies feast on other biting bugs likes mosquitoes and flies, and soon found their alighting on my knee or the hull of my kayak while out paddling was akin to having a protective mascot—my own little pet dragon.

I go to gather ripe red mulberries and search for sweet juneberries, like fairy sized apples, ready to pick down at my forest pond. I spot a Common Whitetail Skimmer dragonfly hawking back and forth across an ecotone of shoreline. All four iridescent wings move independently, so that a dragonfly can actually fly backwards like a hummingbird, hover, and fly in six different planes or directions. Damselflies differ from dragonflies in size and wing structure, the main differences being that damselflies have more narrow attachments of their four wings to their thorax, land more often, and fold their wings up straight when they do so. They are usually slower fliers, unlike some dragonflies that can fly at speeds of 45 miles per hour. The wings of a dragonfly are so efficient that their structure and movement have been studied by NASA's aerodynamic scientists and engineers. This amazing predator is also "all eyes" and can see a full 360 degrees.

Creatures of water, land, and air, dragonflies can take as little as 36 days or up to ten years to mature from their underwater nymph stage to flying adults depending on the species. It's not surprising then that cultures worldwide have used the dragonfly symbolically, gifting it meanings surrounding change. Many people view the butterfly as the metaphor for transformation, but to me, the dragonfly represents the more natural, long and gradual changes that must occur along the way. Maybe the image of the dragonfly is less sweet compared to butterflies, but some powerful and symbolic message in their fierce and flighty behavior resonates in me.

Beside the pond where I gather red mulberries I come upon a firefly resting under a leaf, no doubt spent from the previous evening's magical light show. I hear a buzz behind me and there an adult female dragonfly dips its forked tail into the pond several times in a straight line toward the center, laying eggs for a next generation, securing some sort of immortality.

Gathering watercress and wild mint nearby, I spot the leftover cast remains of a complete dragonfly exoskeleton still attached to a blade of cattail leaf. The dragonfly nymph, or sub adult, when it's ready, climbs out from the water, cracks the back of its thorax, and emerges from its exoskeleton as part of the final molt of incomplete metamorphosis. This type of metamorphosis is also referred to as "instar stages". The dragonfly's wing pads, having been growing year by year, slowly begin to spread and the once dull brownish insect takes on colors ranging from emerald green to turquoise and black. The dragonfly follows an urge that demands waiting while their newly shimmering and resplendent wings dry to be ready to take flight, completely vulnerable to anything that may prey on them.

Obviously, climbing up out of their home into another world, shedding their last layers of exoskeleton and risking everything to spread their wings is a natural act. The process is one of instinct. Then suddenly there is an entirely new way of being, flying on gossamer wings, witness to the amazing color and light here in our middle world. Theirs is a transition from water to air, from one element to another, from one place to the next.

How many times during our own lives do we make our own transitions? Birth. Growing up. Life changes. Death. As I write this I have a mother passing, in hospice right now. I visit her at night when the rest of the family is gone, spending the night holding her hand, wondering if she is scared. My teenage son just graduated high school a year early from Naples Central High and is headed off to Paris for a year as part of Rotary International. It takes courage to leave what is comfortable, to journey into the unknown or emerge as something unknown. It takes courage to take flight and venture off into someplace totally foreign to everything you've known. I can't help but wonder if even a dragonfly nymph senses a new journey, one filled with new light and features.

Hic sunt dragones, Latin for "Here Be Dragons" is an old world phrase credited to ancient mapmakers who used such markings to indicate places that were unknown, possibly dangerous, but above all—full of mystery and in need of exploration. There are few places in the world like that today, and yet the meaning sticks. Maybe it is because so much of the world, and so much about life, is still full of awe and mystery.

Transformation is a cycle of life, full of risk and fear of the unknown. Mysterious. Here be dragons: Vagrant Darter, Flame Skimmer, and Banded Pendant on a breath of summer rose. They are the daring small creatures which venture out into a new world, moving on. *Hic sunt dracones* might be an area right in own backyards, and at all the crossroads of our lives; a place of left behind castings where, given courage and faith, we experience those clear-veined and jeweled wings in flight as part of the natural order of things.

End of Summer Blessings

Much of August was spent teaching writing through Writers & Books, inspiring children to put their magical ideas into words and on to paper. The children never fail to teach me more than I expect about the world, about words, about what kids really need to know. During Outdoor Writers and Where's Walden Camp, my program cohort, Edgar, and I spent a good deal of time teaching the kids about gratitude for the earth and all our blessings—from the elements to the plants, from the animals to the moon. Sharing gratitude is an amazing way to begin each day, in appreciation for all the earth gives us.

Earth teach us thankfulness, like a prairie dog with its paws folded together as it greets the morning sun.

This year I gave up some of my notions about identifying everything; kids don't really want to classify nature stem by stem and bug by bug. They aren't interested in knowing that the salamander they found is actually a newt in its immature red eft stage, a developmental process during which the animal becomes terrestrial for a time before re-developing into an aquatic adult. First things first; the kids want to know the salamander as Steve. They want to make friends with the animal, build a relationship, connect with it on some level. They want to make nature kin.

Earth teach us to listen, the way a mountain catches the whispers of the wind and passes its message to leaves on the trees, as song notes for the wing'd, and in the tone of creek water as it splashes by.

Troops of darner and skipper dragonflies are gathering, preparing for migrations south. Monarch butterflies aren't the only insects that travel great distances; other butterflies like mourning cloak, cabbage whites, and common buckeyes migrate too. Many true bugs migrate—potato leafhoppers and the large milkweed bug, for instance. I once read a report by an airplane pilot describing an amazing cloud of bugs flying through the stratosphere. Imagine that. And there are different types of insect migration, such as altitude migrations and seasonal development migrations. Last spring, when our area was aflutter with millions of red admiral butterflies, we were experiencing a rare irruptive migration caused by changing weather patterns, like those of painted lady butterflies during El Nino years. Invasive insects, because they're not from the region and rarely have any predators to keep their populations in check, migrate here too. The emerald ash borer and the hemlock tree destroyer—the tiny wooly adelgid—are just two examples. Opportunists will expand their territory if nothing is there to keep them in check.

Earth teach me to accept the things I cannot change, the courage to change the things I can, and the heart to respect all life and not just my own.

The grape harvest has begun, at least for some of the early varieties of grapes. The season is a good two weeks early and according to the Cornell Cooperative Extension and viticulturists in the region, the unseasonably hot dry weather of this past July (the hottest on record) is the reason. Several vineyards in the area were affected by the late spring frost and will have reduced harvests, but many other farms missed the damage and benefited from the summer heat. Grape harvest means it's pie season already, but not until the Concord grape pie pinchers get their fingers rolling over the purple orbs like prayer beads.

Earth teach us to persevere, as the tree that leans over the gully year after year, holding its roots strong into the shale cliff sides continues to lift it limbs against gravity and raise them skyward.

"Ba-bubba-ba, dang-a-dang-dang, ding-along-ding, blue moon..." croon The Marcels in their hit song of the 1950s. August 31ˢᵗ is the second full moon of the month and is labeled a blue moon. By more technical definitions, a blue moon occurs only when there are four full moons in a season. Since the following full moon for September falls after the Equinox, our end of August moon isn't true enough to be blue. There are typically twelve full moons that match our twelve months of the year, but a solar year actually has eleven extra days, so every so often we get an extra moon. Since this one isn't technically a blue moon, maybe we should call it a purple moon instead, in honor of the early approaching grape season? Despite any confusion with the rhetoric, tides will swell and the big bright moon will still rise and as the darkness tiptoes closer and closer to mark the end of each day, we look to the night sky for other celestial features like the summer triangle—Deneb, Vega, and Altair in the southern sky.

Earth teach us to see live sustainably, to understand our connection to nature, to the stars, to one another, like the intricate living system we all are.

I recently had a conversation with a fellow about hydrofracking. He said you cannot stop progress; you can't fight the economics of it. I swore I was talking to the Once-ler right out *The Lorax.* We are at a critical point with legislation right now—will we let the natural gas industry pour toxins into the deep underground, create poisonous brines, and irreversibly threaten clean water in New York State, or not? I live near Rte. 53, a road that leads south into Pennsylvania. Sometimes, I swear, I can feel the earth shaking from here. If the governor signs a bill allowing this unethical activity I feel as if I will have to keep watch atop the hill, craning my neck to see when the rigs start coming, to fight against their trespass. Or I could join the grassroots movement, We Are Seneca Lake, and in an act of protest and civil disobedience to protect our Finger Lakes, get arrested. I think I will (and I did).

Earth teach us that we can speak our voice and be heard. That people can, once in a blue moon, make a difference. That we can respect your abundance and not abuse you. That we learn to recognize within our hearts that we are your kin, and so be filled with gratitude.

Bolts from the Blue

Flash! The old adage that lightning never strikes twice in the same place is a fallacy.

Summer here has been unseasonably hot and dry, again; a forecast climate scientists tell us is what global warming looks like. Despite the dryness, thunderstorms still pass through.

I recently lost my computer modem, Wi-Fi, and phone service to lightning, the force of which actually blew the wires straight out of the phone jack, melted the plastic, and blackened the wall. Just days before, poet Michael Czarneki's uninsured home burned to the ground—he and his family lost everything. Because I've lost too many modems and telephones to count, I know firsthand that lightning often strikes twice in the same place. I don't know what caused the Czarneki home to burn to ashes, but given the blackened wall, I realize mine could have easily been next.

Lightning is a potent negative charge in a cloud that can form many branches called stepped leaders, invisible to the eye until Zap! they connect with a positive charge from a positively charged item on earth streaming upward to connect to the leader; cloud-to-ground lightning is a charged event that happens quickly, before the flash of lightning actually reaches our eyes. If you recall basic science— opposites attract. Ice droplets inside the cloud are required for thunder and lightning to form. Positive electrons move to the top of the cloud while negative electrons gather at the bottom. The stepped leader is negatively charged and attracted to a positive charge down below from a tree, telephone pole, hill, lake, or open area (one reason why getting out of a storm requires avoiding such places). The cloud-to-ground lightning is an intensely luminous series of return strokes from land upwards.

I was standing in the horse pasture a few weeks back, calling for my pony as a storm was coming in. Lightning was crashing above and at my feet, the electric fence was sparking off the ground. If I had hair it probably would have been standing on end. I decided it wasn't a safe place, as my wise pony apparently already had, quickly retreating to the shed where I found him.

Flashes within the clouds are cloud-to-cloud lightning, and heat lightning is simply lightning happening somewhere further afield and too far for us to hear its thunderous booming. The other night a fresh bloom of bright green katydids buzzing around the porch light called me outdoors and I saw heat lightning flashes against a clear and starry sky. Positive lightning happens too, but that's another story. Probably the most amazing thing about all the thunder and flash is the fact that without it, earth would be doomed. According to NASA, there are approximately 44 cloud-to-ground lightning events every second on planet earth (sometimes more). Most of these weather events occur in the tropics.

Lightning maintains the electrical balance of the earth. The planet as a whole is negatively charged and is always giving that charge up to the positively charged atmosphere. The atmosphere is not a good conductor, so without thunderstorms rumbling and roiling and constantly flashing back at us, earth would lose its electrical balance in about five minutes flat. Flash!

Just as critical to our planet, lightning breaks up nitrogen in the air allowing nitrogen to enter soil via rain. Another chemical constituent associated with thunderstorms, that clear smell akin to a green apple and metal, is actually ozone. In the upper atmosphere, ozone is critical for protecting life on this planet from the sun's harmful rays. In the lower troposphere, ozone is a pollutant typically caused by human-made smog.

Wings flap out thunder and bolts of lightning shoot from the Thunderbird's eyes in Native American Mythology. One legend says that the powerful Thunderbird carries messages to the Great Spirit and is a beast to avoid angering. Like the legendary Thunderbird, hawks, vultures and eagles often ride the warm updrafts that can precede the formation of the anvil-topped cumulus clouds of thunderstorms.

Boom! Lightning contains up to a billion volts of electricity that can be random, unpredictable, bolts from the blue seeking only one thing—a path of least resistance. The fact that humans have been able to harness electricity is astounding, but like energy from the sun, there is an endless supply—at least until the end of life as we know it.

Together, our earth and our atmosphere are a finely-tuned and miraculous system, constantly striving for homeostasis. Realizing that earth and sky are involved in such a strongly fused and passionate relationship, in a dance that is at times violent, reaching, and charged, on a planet that is so alive and intensely complex, is enough to set me back on my heels for serious contemplation— something easier to do off-line and out of contact when the whole communication shebang has been struck and on hold.

How to Savor the Last Dregs of Summer (and lick the pan clean)

1. When you first notice the sun's azimuth growing lower, adjust the brim of your hat to match the angle of light and ignore it.

2. Although you may ignore the fact that summer is getting hotter, weather everywhere more severe, and climate change is happening...lower your carbon footstep anyway: hang out the laundry, bring reusable bags to the store (wish I could remember this one), buy a solar panel if you can afford it.

3. Reach both hands beneath the weeds in the garden and pull out an overly large zucchini. Bring it in the kitchen and swear you will cook it for dinner.

4. Take a walk in the woods after dark without a flashlight; look for the gleaming firefly larvae in the leaf litter, shining foxfire (bioluminescent fungi) on old logs, and glowing Jack-o' lantern mushrooms. Try calling in a barred owl by giving the guttural cry: "who cooks for you? Who cooks for you all?"

5. Go blueberry picking at a local farm or pick wild blackberries. Come home and make jelly all in the same day.

6. Pick wildflowers along a dirt road or in the fields. Gather armfuls of Queen Ann's Lace, black mahogany seed stems of curly dock, cattails, goldenrod, and black-eyed Susan. Arrange them in a large vase. Or recycle some of those phone books as

flower presses and collect blossoms to decorate bookmarks, cards, even photo frames.

7. In the morning, put your bathing suit on under your clothes even if you are going to work (especially if you are going to work). Carry a towel with you all day and be ready for the moment—even if it's just to turn on the hose and dance underneath it.

8. Listen for the last calls of migratory birds, the clatter of flickers, the chatter of tree swallows, the lyrical songs of white throated sparrows passing through.

9. Take down your hummingbird feeders but replace them with finch feeders and enjoy the lemon colors of goldfinches in full bloom.

10. Sit at one of your local restaurant's front porches. Order a fancy drink (it need not be alcoholic). Waste some time watching the world go by.

11. Pack a picnic and visit an area park or beach you've missed this year. Leave all your communication gadgets at home and enjoy being in the moment, in nature.

12. Watch the sun set and linger till long after dark. Look for constellations like Corona Borealis, Cygnet the Swan, or the Little Dipper.

13. Camp out in the backyard with the kids (if they need motivation, tell them you just treated the house for a flea infestation and they need to stay out for 12 hours but not to worry, you have marshmallows....)

14. Investigate young milkweed plants for signs of newly hatched monarch butterfly caterpillars or look under milkweed leaves for tiny yellow monarch eggs. If you don't have any milkweed this year, set aside a wild area of the yard for next year—I have plenty of seed.

15. Challenge yourself with one more summer adventure - anything from backpacking on the Finger Lakes Trail to getting up one of the area's amazing waterfall gullies, kayaking or sailing on one of the Finger Lakes, or even heading up to New York's Adirondacks to hike a High Peak.

16. Make a list of the top 5 things you are most thankful for. Be amazed that nothing on the list includes technology, consumer goods, signature vehicles, or stuff.

17. Unplug yourself (and the family) for an entire day. If you don't know what to do review this list and then go out and enjoy the deepening of summer; the richness of a season consumed with real abundance, the type worth counting your blessings for.

AUTUMN

September Strands

September is spider webs. Every morning long silver strands reach from roof edge to doorway. Perfectly designed nets are strung across the porch railings and in the woods, small discs shimmer between tree branches. The most active and talented web makers this time of year are the orb-weaving Argiope, or garden spider—a large yellow and black spider whose females grow three to five inches in length. Each night the Argiope devours all strands of her spiral web from the previous day, and then spins a new spectacular piece of work to catch her evening dinner. As the month progresses she will feel the close of the season, the hurriedness to finish all that is left to be done, lay an egg, and die. The egg will hatch over 1,000 spiderlings which overwinter in their snug egg sac, waiting till spring to balloon away into the world on gossamer threads.

September is sunflowers slumping their shoulders, heads of falling yellow hair, bent as if in prayer, preparing seeds our winter songbirds can enjoy. In September the curtain is raised; the unveiling of chlorophyll pigments of orange carotene, red anthocyanin and yellow xanthophyll in leaves take center stage. September is monarch butterflies and troops of green darner dragonflies gathering, preparing to migrate before a first frost drops crickets in the fields like stones, leaving us a sudden silence.

We live in a region where climate and season dictate the instincts and changes in the natural world, but how much doesseason and climate affect us? Are we not all engaged in this last flamboyant act? Seasonally the grapes round and ripen and pie stands appear along the roadsides. Some Fire God within my woodstove lures me into hauling and stacking wood for a charismatic mystery and warmth I will be smitten by. Tomatoes are stewed and canned, the last of the basil is picked, and chickens are culled. We are shaped by the seasons, the shortening of days; strands of the natural world that pull with a powerful tug. But does the web feel the pluck of climate change here?

I spiraled back to McCarthy, Alaska, this summer and basked in sweet balsam poplar-scented air surrounded by ice capped peaks and rivers leaping like the backs of whales. I used to hike the Kennicott and Root Glaciers when I lived there, and although I was deliriously happy to get my crampon-footed boots back onto that ice, I didn't fail to notice the large tarn lake that wasn't there before and the receding of this living, breathing being of ice and rock. But that's what glaciers do, they change, change the landscape and their own forms, right?

One poet there, who spent five years teaching Inuit children above the Arctic Circle, talked about the melting permafrost, about polar bears coming into the village looking for food, about entire communities losing their homes due to climate change. All around me writers wondered how to help the call to action, how to stop our rapid change in the planetary thermostat. I grappled with the enormity of such a task and then sat and just took in the sublime that was still here around this little frontier town. I saw how the cabins there had changed—solar panels on roofs now (not that there was any other source of power), a community garden (free for picking), and signage to remind everyone how precious their stream source of clean drinking water was to them (a water hole I visited in a ritual of gratitude at the end of each day on my way back to my tent). Driving in McCarthy was practically forbidden (just getting a permit for a car in the village was pricey) but there was a shuttle van. I saw that small, simple solutions, strand upon strand, might add up.

September, like our lives, strides forward with accelerating speed and blinding busyness. Should we not all rush to finish with all this growth and production? And then I see the bright yellow side-striped spider, eight long legs nearly orange, just waiting. The labyrinth she strung across my pasture fence last night is one of her last acts of beauty before the season ends. It reminds me how connected all life is with its environment, its seasons, and its climate. I wonder what webs we might weave that could reflect such perfect grace if we truly took to heart the old saying attributed to Chief Seattle, about how whatever we do to the web affects the web of life, the strands of which we are all part of.

Rob's Trail: A Watershed Movement

Gravity. It lures raindrops groundwards. It pulls, coaxes, and draws drowsy droplets gone cohesive into rivulets, creek-lets, or gullies towards a larger body of water below. It also the tugs at my legs downhill. From the top of Route 15A and Old South Bald Hill Road, along the high ridge between Canadice and Hemlock Lakes, the Nature Conservancy's trail, named for Rob van der Stricht, has had one path that, like a raindrop landing just east of center, rolled down to Canadice Lake. Now, nearly eight years later, a new extension on the west side of the ridge leads down to Hemlock Lake. This connector trail makes for a rare lake-to-lake path between two of the only undeveloped of the eleven Finger Lakes. Both lakes are sources of drinking water for Rochester. The two entrances at the highland of Rob's Trail mark the nearly precise point where the watersheds of each of these pristine lakes begin.

The Hemlock Lake extension sets out in a shrub field of silky dogwood and hawthorn but quickly enters a hillside community of sugar maple, chestnut oak, hickory and hornbeam. When some friends and I first stepped into the woods I heard the call of a bald eagle to the south, and was touched by the knowledge that this long and wild-edged lake was a place of hope that saw the return of the first nesting bald eagles in New York State back in the 1960s. Further down the trail, winding along a gully shaded in towering hemlock, we came across moosewood trees and a family of larch.

This is a trail to visit all autumn long. First the maples spin hues of brilliant reds. Then the hickory turn to russets. The finale is the golden glow of larch, when the witch hazel will just be blooming.

Solid and well placed bridges, as well as woodland crafted stepping stones, crisscross the gullies and feeder streams along the journey. After a summer of so little rain it is difficult to recall the usefulness of such rocky beds. The course ways and streams lack a certain charm when only slate remains without the sparkle of water, nor is there the skipping rushing melody of water headed downward to the lake, but I know those waters will return. All these gullies scratch into the back of the hillside, waiting, for a reason. Beyond the throughfall of rain toward gullies are stony and well-drained soils. Any rainwater that doesn't adhere to soil particles to be sucked up by rootlets and transpired from leaves back to the sky will percolate downward, eventually reaching the water table and then the lake. Heavier storm water goes skittering down the gully ways bringing along whatever chances to be surfaced there—fallen leaf debris, mayfly exoskeletons, hickory nuts, sediments, and anything else awaiting decomposition.

What keeps these lakes clean and only aging succesionally ever so slowly is a lack of inputs of excess nutrients and organic wastes from farms and residences, not that they weren't once numerous; both lakes hosted cottages and open farmland about 150 years ago. In a watershed moment all its own, the City of Rochester purchased the lakes for a water supply (now under the jurisdiction of the DEC) and began to buy out the summer cottage goers. By the 1940s the lake shore was returning to an ecotone, forests began to succeed former sheep farms, and a rare treasure for this region arced back in time leaving two side by side lakes void of development. The lakes sparkled in return.

When we eventually drop down to the bottom of Rob's Trail and hit the shoreline of Hemlock, we take a break from walking and visit the lake edge awhile. I see only one small water craft, a good half mile off, across the eastern shore. The lake is quiet but for the wind. We skip stones. Rest on the warm rocks. I think of who Rob van der Stricht must have been. He was called "a gentle giant." He loved birding. He was a conservation activist, world traveler and former board chair of the Nature Conservancy. I can't help but think that Rob would be pleased with the way his namesake trail showcases such a model watershed and its prerequisite for clean sparkling water, wooded hillsides, rooted gullies, and gravity.

The Balance of Northern Time

"Wake up with the birds. Go to sleep with the birds. Wake up with the birds...." on and so forth was written across my friend's wall in black marker. The rhythm of it was enticing, both literally and figuratively. But this seasonal stretch of long days that dawned with the calls of phoebes, towhees, and warblers, and closed curtain with the notes of thrushes and the nocturnal chorus of frogs and toads, is sliding away. Since the Summer Solstice, we have lost a minute of light a day for the first month. The pace of light loss accelerates and now two minutes per day is sliced off diurnal time as we reach the Autumn Equinox on September 21st. Tiny green tree frogs and bullfrogs have grown hoarse and sleepy and insects now fill the void (lest there be silence too soon). Now katydids and crickets whir, chirp, buzz, and trill. The occasional sawyer beetle adds its chaw to the humming siren of night. Honey bees stock up on liquid sweetness. True silence comes after the first hard frost. The rhythm of light versus night incites change.

Circadian rhythms are natural cycles life attunes itself to in places on the Earth where daylight hours shift seasonally. Everything and everyone is affected, from the fungi and cyanobacteria in the soil to plants, insects, birds, and animals—like us. Despite the laggard but resultant solar cooling effect, it is actually the shortening length of daylight, more so than the falling temperatures, that signal trees to shut down their green chlorophyll factories, seal off their petiole stems, drop leaves. The low angles of ultraviolet light, at the far ends of the light spectrum, inform dragonflies to troop together and prepare for their migration, much like monarch butterflies do.

Our songbirds, well fed on a northern summer diet of bugs and ripe seeds, feel the obvious shift of the season and slowly disappear for winter in the far southern USA and the tropics of Central America. How they know when to return to the Little Lakes of Upstate New York, or anywhere north, is still a great mystery wrapped up in weather shifts, the Earth's magnetic forces, and other factors scientists are still studying. Somehow, even the blue-grey gnatcatchers recognize this change down at the Equator; they know when the Northern Hemisphere begins to tilt again toward the sun on its year-long, elliptical orbit. And each year their migration is monitored shows them heading further and further North.

Right now, even as Earth moves a bit closer to the sun on its 365 day circular journey around it, Earth also begins a slow tilt away from the sun, slanting slowly toward the shortest hours of daylight for the northern hemisphere during the Winter Solstice. The approaching Autumnal Equinox is time to take the in the hush from the tasks of summer, to welcome back the darkness that call us to rest.

Despite this temporary balance of light vs. dark in our lives, the 24-hour-day is not an exact clock in relation to the actual spin of the Earth—a speed which has us moving at about 1,000 miles per hour. And time does change: large earthquakes like the one in Japan in 2011 actually caused an estimated increase in our mph spinning speed by about 1.8 milliseconds per day. For so many of us, life does seem to speed ahead at an accelerating rate. Karen Thompson Walker's novel, *The Age of Miracles*, depicts a story of life on our planet where the spin is not speeded up (as it seems to be doing in reality), but slowed to such a degree that darkness and light last days and weeks instead of hours. People become fiercely divided over whether to stick to Natural time or continue to use the traditional 24 hour clock. It's an interesting notion, natural time versus clock time, one we Northerners normally adjust to month by month and season by season.

Think about what a rare calamity of planetary measures causes leaves to change color and squirrels to gather acorns. Think about it! Think about what an anomaly it is you can adhere to a planet spinning so fast while orbiting the sun while at the same time wobbling on an invisible axis that makes things as you know them— ripening apples, spiders laying egg sacks before their lives expire, luscious loads of fall squashes—all possible. It's enough to cause you want to hang on tight, linger over a lick of fresh gathered honey, and try to slow it all down.

The Dance of Change

Trees are dancers shifting colors, giving a splash of bloom and brightness to the landscape, reaching up and outward in seeming imperceptibility to a song too slow for our ears to hear but heartfelt all the same. Humans are creatures of a faster pace, with short lives and quicker moves. Trees seem solid and rigid. So permanent. Still, one can look at trees and witness sublime trunk and branching forms akin to a dancer's pose. Sometimes two trees are entwined in a waltz or embrace, or one tree appears to be in a yoga-like position. Tree silhouettes show character, be it jovial or haunting, as well as form. But trees aren't static beings entirely frozen in motion.

No. Trees can move.

Trees bend to the wind. They turn with the seasons. They reach for the sun and dance through time. Trees also walk in what is better known as Range Migration, when conditions change. And many of our familiar tree species are beginning to migrate northward with the warming of our climate.

Trees move by means of seed dispersal variations that involve wind, or by animal mechanisms (such as seeds being eaten and shat or buried elsewhere) to spread their progeny. If a seed ends up someplace conducive to the soil, water, and climate needs of the species, it will grow. And so it does. As the earth warms, currently estimated to be at a rate of 5-6 degrees Celsius by the end of this century, tree species have to face the heat as well.

Sugar maples are marching farther North. So are the firs, pines, hemlock, and yellow birch, to name a few. According to the USDA, the rate of migration is about 50-100 hectares per century. Here, in the Finger Lakes, our autumns are a vibrant tapestry of colorful, but masked, chlorophyll pigments unveiled as each leaf dies to ready itself for winter. That is a grand dance all its own. Our sugar and red maples are most notable on our autumn landscape for their robust hues in dry years, and phoenix-type flames in wet ones. We look forward to, savor, and reminisce on such views.

Life, though, is all about change and all about movement. From seedling to bud, from blossom to seed, from season to season, year to year, one life gives way to the next. Dominant species transform, sometimes because insect and parasites attack very specifically (that is how the elm, once a vital part of Seneca culture, was eradicated from the region). Some species are pushed out by invasives that overtake an area quickly. A majority of the eradications experienced these days are human-caused: we accidently move seeds and parasites through the globalization of humankind. And we destroy habitat. We alter water patterns. We build and conquer and submit nature to our will. We change ecological conditions through our actions and our movement. That is our dance.

Some 400 million years ago, this landscape was tropical with towering mosses of *Lycopodium* mosses and horsetail *Equisetum*— then the size of trees—as well as an enormous inland sea. Later, the mile high glaciers, less than 10,000 or so years past, were followed by an unhurried transformation to a temperate forest wilderness.

There was a gradual warming over time. Once we had chestnut tree giants (who disappeared due to blight) and hundreds-year-old oaks, white pine, and larch, cut for lumber and clearing. What we are facing now is just as impactful. We are the initiators of the change.

The fact that sugar maples and other species are here in this area, during this time, is a blessing for all of us to enjoy. But trees are movers and adapters, species are slowly pushing north. We should wonder what sort of plants, crops, animals, and breathless array of autumn colors our next generation will waltz to in time? In this long, delicate movement of human evolution, what dance of color and bloom and leaf change will our decedents see on the landscape, season by season and year by year?

I don't believe it's entirely too late to change the lyrics or the melody we are dancing to.

Giving Grapes The Slip

The sun slips to a lower azimuth in the sky. Shadows lengthen and the days begin to crisp around the edges. For the majority of autumns this past decade I slipped grape skins by hand, one grape at a time, separating slick innards from small stones for local grape pie makers like Jeni. I pinched grapes like counting prayer beads: Hail Mary full of Grace. The Lord is with thee. Blessed are Thou amongst women. Other times I said a Tibetan Mantra that fit the sport better—Om Mani Padme Hum. Over and over I took whole clusters into my hands watching each tray of grapes slowly slip down in size; each fruit a Mani, a prayer wheel my fingers circled round.

This will be the first year I choose not to slip any grapes at all. Slipping grapes is time-consuming, hard work. But a job I will miss none the less.

Making a grape pie is a complicated process. Visitors out touring Naples's autumn colors, wines, art, and fall festivals in these hills are intrigued enough to purchase a grape pie, roadside, as a souvenir. From pie stands like Jeni's, Mom's, and Monica's Pies (to name a few), many women here have supported their families by making and selling these signature pies, not to mention preserving the legacy of Concord grapes. I'm a slipper, not a baker, but the seasonal work has been necessity for me too. I worked tray after tray of Concord grapes to pay my property taxes and to purchase winter wood. Thoreau's words echoed in my head: "I went to the woods because I wished to live deliberately, to front only the essential facts of life..." Despite John Henry size tales of women who could pinch a tray of grapes in under an hour, it still almost always took me closer to two. I would go as fast as I could but it's wrist-hurting, back-aching work. Should I complain, I was told the Mennonite and Amish women nearby would slip a tray for half the money I get. Om Mani Padme Hum! What I would really, really like to see at the Grape Festival is a grape slipping contest. Grape slippers do not get the recognition they deserve!

The process of slipping grapes is this: grape gut goo is pinched by hand out into one bucket while the skins are kept separate, gathered in the palm, while pinching steadily until you cannot fit another dripping purple envelope between your fingers. Then your stiff claw is opened and dark stained skins are plopped into a separate bowl. Grape goop is cooked, strained of seeds, and the skins, needed for color and tartness, are added to the pie right before it slips into the oven.

What slips away all these Septembers, all these grape pie seasons, are the same things I clutched all those years with a desire to live a simpler life, one wringing with the idea of self-sufficiency. It seems that simplicity is far harder to hold; simplicity slips so easily between one's fingers while life's demands bang on the door incessantly, full of want.

Snakes slip their skins, insects their exoskeletons, young trees their tender bark for something creviced, rough, and hard. In Celtic Mythology the Silkie seal slips its skin and becomes human, but lives in longing for the sea. Maybe we all keep slipping into something else while longing for what was left behind?

While pinching grapes I would slip back into moments of pleasure in the season, cool breezes and a clear sky, the fragrant smell of ripe grapes, a saturation of seasonal color in a season that slipped into handful after handful of grape bunches until I was sticky up to my elbows. Yellow jackets came to get drunk on the elixir, buzzing Om Mani Padme Hummmmmm.

But I would also agonize over my sore thumbs working, my nails blackening and softening in the acidity of the grapes. After a bit I'd begin to wonder if I would ever finish the trays I brought home. Maybe the real beauty of the season will be in letting the ghosts of autumn past slip away, in order to slip into something new.

Nineteen Things October Brings

1. The haunting screech of a grey fox below the pasture, awakening me in pre-dawn's starlight-dressed hours, luring me to get up and see the rare convergence of Venus, Mars, Jupiter, and Mercury, all below Leo in the Eastern sky.

2. Decay's sweet, aromatic, and funky smell as bacteria and fungi break down fallen leaves and other duff, recycling it all beautifully back into the soil.

3. A discovery of mushrooms in the woods with names like dead man's fingers, witch's butter, red tree brain, monkey ear, turkey tail, and poison pie.

4. Mysteries of seed dispersal via sticky beggar ticks and burrs revealed in the dog's thick fur—and getting out the scissors to deal with them all.

5. Garlic tastings, Saturdays, at Fruition Seeds, savoring Rose du Var, Purple Glazer, Inchelium Red and other heirloom bulbs. Trying to remember which was nutty or buttery or less sulfuric, knowing I have a fall garden bed for garlic ready to be planted.

6. The sudden spell to stand still and savor the brilliant blue midday sky over a tapestry of trees in seasonal tresses.

7. The hardening, warty-skinned fruits of last summer's labor – spaghetti squash, butternut, pumpkin and acorn—to cure and put by for fall and winter stews.

8. A feeling deep in my bones that I need to take one more paddle on Canadice or Hemlock Lakes to admire the reflection of fall colors on water, of water lighting the air, of the autumn air itself.

9. Winding country roads into small towns like Naples with pop-up tents selling pies in flavors of Concord grape, pumpkin, apple, and elderberry; swearing that if I sell pies at a stand this fall I will eat at least one whole pie myself.

10. Hoards and herds of wooly bear caterpillars crossing the roads, remembering the chart my son and I made during his preschool year to investigate any truth to the folklore about the caterpillar's black bands predicting the coming winter, and realizing how many winters have passed; my son grown and at Cornell now....

11. Digging for medicinal roots of goldenseal, elecampane, and Echinacea for winter's healing tinctures against colds, cough, and flu.

12. Northern Spy, Lady, Jonathan, Winesap, Gala, Honeycrisp, Ida Red and many more for eating, baking, and cider—fresh or as fermented brew.

13. Notice of the camouflage, the skills, and keen eyes of bow hunters headed back out for a late afternoon hunt and wishing I were one of them too.

14. Imagining great Halloween costumes I will never have enough occasions to wear: Persephone, the Snow Queen, or maybe a Seneca Lake Salt Mine storing hydrofracking waste?

15. My daughter's high school soccer games; me wrapped in a blanket and dreaming of a hot dinner while kettles of hawks and vultures circle the thermals overhead, preparing for migration.

16. Chocolate.

17. Not so much a longing for the stacking and finishing of getting wood in, but a loss for the feel of that wood smell, the curl of its smoke, the deep inner radiance of a woodstove's light and heat as the daylight hours fold in.

18. The stacking of scratchy, and clover-scented hay for the horse in the cobwebby barn.

19. A traditional setting out of an extra plate for Halloween's harvest dinner in memory of my ancestors, for those who have recently passed away, and for the one I miss whose echo of grateful prayers still whisper in my ears.

All My Relations
(A Halloween Story in Two Parts)

If you want to see wildlife the best place to go isn't the woods but the road. On one morning commute to Canandaigua I spot Skunk dressed up with a Mohawk along the centerline, her musky odoriferous smog greeting me a mile before I ever encounter her body. I count Raccoon (squished), Doe (roadside), Squirrel (dead center in my lane) and another animal totally unrecognizable in a pile of blood and guts as I zoom by at a speed too ghastly for the early hour of the day. And I'm not the only car that has raced by these animals without stopping. We are all so immune to our daily destruction of those who share our community that I wonder if even apathy can explain it. It's just plain scary.

Google Images of earth began to show only developments and sword-like criss-crossings of dirt roads, main roads, and highways. The animals who shared the land with us had to contend constantly with our eagerness to get someplace, in usually a great big hurry. Animals had places to go too, obviously, or we wouldn't have seen them on the road.

I've hit quite a few animals and I've been known to pick up roadkill on occasion: a fresh hit grouse that's not too banged up has gone into the pot and once, when I thought I'd have a grouse dinner after a huge gust of wind sent a bird pummeling into my car radiator, I ended up nursing what turned out to be a screech owl. The kids and I released it back into the wild after a few days and pet store mice later. One of the most memorable poems I've ever heard was about a woman picking up a dead fawn on the road and utilizing every bit of it, down to the lard it made for pie crust. I've also collected porcupine quills for earrings off a road kill, [moved a coyote off Route 53 I planned to pick up after work and have processed for its pelt (did you take it?),] and eaten road kill deer that, when the cost of car repairs was over, ended up being some pretty pricey steak.

In some areas, salamander and other amphibian crossings caused such high mortality rates for endangered species that highway departments built amphibian crossing culverts under the roads in an attempt to get these small animals from the woods to their seasonal breeding grounds. It helped some, until their habitats disappeared.

A couple weeks ago I was helping with a Pack Paddle Ski canoe program for ninth-graders at Hemlock Lake. There was a dead raccoon in the middle of the boat access road; the route the school bus would be taking back and forth all day. Much to the other guide's horror, I asked if we could please take the animal off the road before the kids started arriving. The other guide was surprised, even tried to brush off the idea saying, "The kids won't even notice it." I thought some of them would, and worse, that the bus would be running it over again and again all day long. I got out and moved the animal off into the wooded road edge. Two crows in the tree overhead yelled at me, probably afraid I was stealing their lunch.

Some animals wouldn't cross roads at all, and their numbers declined. Wolves needed about 25 square miles of uninterrupted territory, space that grew harder and harder to come by. Grizzly bears didn't care much for paved roads either, so Glacier National Park is now the only living zoo with grizzly bears left in the Lower 48. All the other animals are either in urban zoos or have gone extinct.

Of course, one can talk about the whole food chain involving death and scavengers and the wonder of our well-oiled ecological system; talk about the overpopulation of deer, the dangers of braking for wildlife (something I am not suggesting you do for fear of injuring yourself)—but what about the souls of these living relations? What about grieving amongst the animal's kin? What does leaving the dead in the road say about humankind?

Native Americans believed that the animals were our brothers and sisters. They believed that all the animals—insects, birds, mammals—had messages for us; that Great Spirit worked through them to help us on our journey. The Animal People were our guides in a sense. One can only imagine the cost to our souls with the absence of their presence.

Animals do grieve. I was reminded recently that there are people who don't think animals have souls, people who think only they are worthy of such afterlife-movings-on. I suppose that could explain some of the apathy. But what about grief for the loss of a loved one—isn't that something all beings can relate to? We know that chimpanzees will carry their dead offspring around for days in mourning. We know that elephants will stand vigil over a dead member of the herd; that some animals live a long, long time and some mated pairs, left without their partners, display extreme sorts of grief. Even our pets display grief over the loss of an owner or stable mate, and we for them. Aren't we all animals too?

If we were to consider the souls and feelings of animals and their importance to our own souls, think about how our behaviors might change. After all, what would a Council of All Beings say about our doings? One could get into a whole slew of environmental and animal rights issues here but for now, I'll just stick to the road. Of course, moving an animal off the road is tricky, gruesome, nasty, gut-wrenching business, but trying to do so (given safety measures like rubber gloves and reflector tape on your jacket) is an act of kindness that could be an act of higher human-kindness as well. Maybe you say a little prayer, tell the animal kin that you are sorry, blow sage smoke over their body and wish them well on their next journey. Maybe it's the least we can do in this fossil fuel age until we can think of gentler ways to live—and be—that takes into account all living things.

The movie, Fantasia II, and Douglas Adam's Hitchhiker's Guide to the Galaxy made unique references to the whales and dolphins trying to warn us of our own demise, giving up, and then disappearing into outer space. It seems like that now, with all the animals gone, that they someone disappeared into the universe. The planet feels colorless and alone.

All Hallows Eve was actually a Pagan, or Druid, holiday in Celtic Lore that honored relatives who had passed away that year. It was believed the veil between the living and the spirit world was thinnest at this time. Tradition involved putting out a plate of dinner for recently deceased family members in case they spirited by. Maybe on All Hallows Eve we could honor and remember *all our relations*, including those we consider so infrequently, those whose bodies we see daily in the road, those who feel our impact the hardest.

Ritual of the Seasons
or, "How Not to Stack Wood"

Three hundred and sixty-five days, give or take one every four years, we circle round the sun and circle round the years in an outward spiral of larger changes. The inward spiral of the seasons is the one that holds us steady. Filled with subtle rituals, seasonal changes help us find balance to keep us grounded enough to face the bigger picture.

Each season has its own design. Autumn goes from ripe to rot, and from gaudy bright to somber sepia. Autumn is for getting the wood in and readying for winter. It is the end of October and the last of the garden has to be brought in, or mulched heavy. I attempt to put the garden to bed before the snow hits, get some garlic planted, dig out the gladiola and canna lily bulbs. But the long list of repairs and things to button up against the winter winds might be better off written on little slips of paper and tied to the thin legs of migrating songbirds for all the good it does me.

I head out to the mound of unstacked firewood and have just gathered a few chunks in my arms when my ears call my eyes up. Like spring in reverse, a flock of red-winged blackbirds are gathered in the cottonwood at the top of the drive, singing a call I've recognized my entire life, only instead of Oka-Reee! they trill against the cold: eeeek-ack! Ok! And all-at-once they flush in a big gust of feathers like a school of fish, and disappear. I don't need to let them go, they just do. I sigh. It will be late February before I hear them again.

Grape pie season merged into apple, French coconut, pumpkin and grapple pies with seamless progression. The pie seller's tents came down. Unraked leaves now muddy the ground. My woodpile beckons; damp, mossy, dirty mixed loaves of carbon begging for care and balance.

There's plenty of advice out there on how to stack wood—a truly seasonal ritual. First time I ever used wood for heat was while at Paul Smiths College in the Adirondacks. I will always remember the forester prof's words of wisdom to my housemate and me: "The secret," he said, "is to move the wood as few times as possible."

A well-stacked pile of wood is said to be a sign that the resident is hard-working and adept; someone who takes pride in their home. Honestly, I've never gotten very good at the stacking part. It seems helpful to have some pallets or boards on the ground. But if you're as clever as I am at creating rickety, slanted ends, then having a couple good braces—be they solid trees or a post put into the ground—is essential.

I've not tried the round house design, where you make a wide circular bottom of logs and keep stacking up into a spiral until you end up with a something that looks like a little hobbit hut. I realize I could tell folks that's what the current heap was intended to be: "Why yes!' I'd say, "that's a roundhouse stack, I saw it in *Mother Earth News*." But instead I dig through the log pile looking for square and flattish pieces to use for ends, stacking blocks of two across by two horizontal to create what I hope will be stable, square ends. The rest of the wood gets stacked between.

I like to take notice of the species of wood I'm stacking, finding the solid oak pieces burn longest and hottest if they are truly dry, hornbeam about the same. The ash works pretty well green or seasoned, and I always have plenty of that. Occasionally I find the dark chippy bark of cherry still with a faint aroma of bitter almond intact.

Then I get to admiring the logs. Several pieces are covered with amazing fungi; turkey tails and little shelf fungi that lie in small layers going up the log like fairy steps. There's also violet toothed polypore, parchments, and wolf's milk slime molds (not a fungi, but actually a protozoa-mold combination). These logs are such things of beauty I don't want to bury them in the stack so I set them aside, or on top, creating odd, but intentional-looking sculptures around the wood pile.

Moisture holding bark gets torn loose. Underneath is another world: the engraved patterns of artistry and livelihood made by bark beetles, their nuptial chambers radiating out from a center point. Another piece has the deeper, punkier channels made by termites, and around the ends, the hyphae of mushrooms create a netting-like a mini forest of trees on a minute scale. Each log holds a community of organisms all its own working in balance to consume and convert what I desire to burn into recycled carbon for the earth.

There are other forms of heat, the fossil fuels that also give off carbon into the atmosphere. Tons of it. But, of course, fossil fuels aren't renewable, and unlike wood, their origin is no longer here to help convert CO_2 back into organic carbon. Wood for heat is not a perfect balance, but better...maybe.

Superstorm Sandy did a number on the tarps covering my wood, and now it's all wet. The situation is far, far worse for others and so I count my blessings. Some people wonder if the ferocity of the storm was just a part of nature, or a sign of earth out of balance, a warning of the effects of global warming on the planet. I wonder often if we humans will get better at shoring up our own ends, demonstrating that in that larger cyclic spiral we know of as change, we can demonstrate that we are hard-working, adept, and take pride in our home planet—that we can find balance, that we can address, and decrease, our out-of-control CO_2 emissions and methane.

I appreciate the cycles of the seasons. Although there's nothing as gratifying as seeing the results of one's labors like having a stoking warm fire in the house on a snowy morning and a few meaty squash in the stew pot, I'm still not ready for the rituals of winter or the bigger spirals of change. I still have to finish stacking the wood and preparing. I have to find this new balance and let go of a season I thought just arrived.

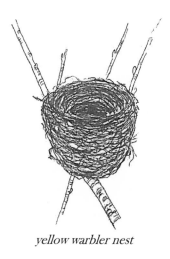

yellow warbler nest

An Unveiling of Autumn Nests

Last night I was weaving a slim cherry branch through the delicate edges of a Northern Oriole's nest left behind from summer. The nest is a pouch of lichen threads and spun cottonwood fluff, or maybe felted cobwebs on a tapestry of mycelium, I don't know, it was gifted to me by my expert birder friend, Sasha, from Finger Lakes Community College. I wanted to hang it over the door in the house I just bought. Carefully threading the twigs through wasn't easy, I don't have a beak and should have used a crochet hook. Still, the pouch is hung, and there is a small fly hook tangled on this branch I gathered alongside Naples Creek.

When the season lets go of all its lush foliage, leaf by leaf, new structures emerge exposing beatific and hidden forms of seasonal, temporary, and transitional shelters; bird nests are among them, but so are the soft fuzz of cocoons like those of the wintering mourning cloak caterpillars, the fragile egg cases of spiders, the goldenrod gall hosting a miniscule wasp larvae, and the hardened thick foam of a praying mantis's ootheca containing hundreds of eggs for next spring.

A nest holds. Nests vary in design.

Bumble bee ground nests decay in the fall, and many in the *Apidae* family don't make it to spring. Squirrels gather bails of leathery oak leaves high in the trees, so that they can. Porcupines use no nests at all.

A nest can be a gathering, or a place to be alone.

In fall I look for bird nests adorned with the scattered bits of colored yarn, the long thick strands of my pony's tail, and fistfuls of hairbrush tangles from my daughter's lovely red locks; these offerings I put out in the spring for the birds in hopes the autumn might unveil colorful works I contributed to in some small way. But I'm at a new piece of property now, out of the woods and on a sunny hillside. There is a bluebird box here (under the twisted flowering pear I think a Buddha statue should be sitting under) with three abandoned blue eggs that, somehow, break my heart.

Nests are left to be windblown. Empty nests are just remains.

There are homes inhabited for shelter from winter, nests for raising young, cocoons passed through as a transition to something else, homes in which to do one's work, homes for settling in and homes for dying in. Cherished gentle shelters or those with memories as ragged as denim fray, each is a moment of time in the ever changing journey called life. Like all things in nature, we too must move from season to season, year to year, and sometimes change the nest we call home in ways physical, mindful, or both.

A nest is for rearing. A nest is for resting. A nest is for calling one home.

Forget the Big Bad Wolf

Little Red Riding Hood goes into the woods. She isn't afraid of any wolf, although she would gladly prefer a wolf over the tiny specks of eight legged arthropods hidden in the brush. These creatures are "questing:" waving about their antennae-like fore thumbs, known as Hollar's organs, to pick up a trace of her CO_2. She is prey, and that is what she needs to be wary of. Both her mother and grandmother complain often that there never used to be ticks here when they were growing up.

The brown dog tick and deer tick have traveled to the Finger Lakes region and beyond without wings, simply by attaching themselves to other animals, birds, and reptiles. Ticks have made slow and steady progress into new territory. Ticks like warm, humid environments and can survive deep freezes well below zero as well as periods of drought. They are nearly indestructible. More significantly, ticks are vectors for a variety of disease-causing pathogens. Most notably in our region is *Borrelia burgdoferi*, the bacteria that causes Lyme disease.

Borrelia bacteria have been on the planet for over a 100 million years. They are highly successful and adaptable, and they move quickly via a tail like structure called flagellum, a mode more unique among bacteria. In their microscopic world they can key in to a variety of hosts and a variety of inner body ecosystems, from joints to organs to the brain, even changing their own genotype to fit the whimsy of opportunity. Borrelial bacteria inhabit areas throughout the globe. There are so many species with so much variability that once you are infected, there is no single cure.

Little Red has heard tales that Lyme is the fault of deer, and the fault of white-footed mice. Red knows better. Although black footed deer ticks require both small and large hosts to complete their nymph-to-adult-egg cycle, ticks are not that picky about who serves them. Neither are the pathogens they carry. And it is the pathogens within their sucking bite that poses the health risk. Pathogens like *Borrelia* that once traveled via large herds of large mammals, now find humans the prominent land animal, and a consummate host. With top level predators eradicated, lowered numbers of birds who eat ticks, and pesticides that kill potential tick-eating insects on the rise, we have fueled the impact of ticks upon ourselves. Just as critical to the paradigm of this new tick culture is the changed dynamics of the ecosystems where we live. We have fragmented forests and meadows, then moved ourselves into these areas. We have warmed our planet. We have altered the climate and the ecology, thus inviting more ticks and their diseases to thrive.

"Our ecological ignorance is one major factor in the emergence of the Lyme epidemic," writes Stephen Buhner, author of *Healing Lyme*. He adds that, "Lyme is not 'just a disease.' Its powerful emergence in our time is a planetary response to human generated ecological disruption."

Before heading out through the woods with her basket, Little Red Riding Hood pulls her socks up over her light colored pant legs (which have been soaked with pyrethrum, or other more serious bug spray). In the basket she brings to Grandma's house are her favorite Lyme treatments: lion's mane, reishi, and turkey tail mushrooms, a tincture of teasel and the invasive Japanese knotweed (the later invaded the region just as the deer tick arrived, and now shows evidence as a treatment to attack the *Borrelia spirochetes*). She also brings essential oils of Labrador tea, juniper, lemon eucalyptus and marjoram to make a body spray to help try to keep the ticks at bay. Little Red Riding Hood is brave, and smart. She adapts to new predators. She lives in a new world.

Still Sitting

I remember a co-teacher at an environmental education center where I worked once who reminded me of the Lorax: all wild hair and beard, short of stature, but large on words. I recall him telling the children how he had spent his Sunday sitting under an oak tree all day. How it was one of the most productive days he had ever had. In all honesty, I thought him lazy. It took me a few years to come to understand the full depth of his meaning.

A hunter sits in quiet observation. All senses humming. The hunter's ears are alert to each scrunch of fallen leaves, the alarm call of a red squirrel, or the wistful whistle of a migrating white-throated sparrow. The early morning hunter may see the moon set before the sunrise. Sitting in nature while the sun or moon incrementally cross the sky is a practice of more than observation, but of patience and mindfulness. You cannot hurry the hunt, nor can you hurry the rise of whichever sky luminary directs you. You must wait. The mental and spiritual benefits of exploring each moment as they come are similar to meditation.

With my Forest School children I have created a routine of Sit Spots, or Still Sitting, as part of our school day, and it seems to be something they look forward to. All around the camp that is our tree-filled classroom they each head off to a spot that is their own special Still Hunting place. In the words of John Muir, "to sit in solitude, to think in solitude, with only the music of the stream and the cedar to break the flow of silence...". Some of the children climb up in the trees, as Muir once famously did to experience a thunder storm. One child lounges along a muscle wood branch like a panther in repose. Others sit banked behind the roots of large trees, or in the opening to a creek-fed meadow of sawgrass and spent goldenrod and asters. I am amazed when I tell them we will try for five minutes of quiet sitting, and they ask for ten.

To go from busy and boisterous mud-jumping, firewood-sawing and games to total silence with 16 or more youngsters is a stunning experience. For a few moments the woods is just the sound of itself, and we become part of its echo. Sometimes a hawk flies over. Or the sound of a peeper frog practicing its call rings in. The sweet scent of the rot of fallen leaves rises. The wind gives a pinch to our cheeks, like what a favorite aunt might do. For some of the children it is time to converse with the trees in a silent tongue we adults have forgotten.

Having taken up hunting last year I understand a new dimension to what stillness in the outdoors involves. The old adage says, it's better to be in my treestand thinking about God, than in church thinking about hunting. Dressed properly for the weather, it is a soothing activity of timeless non-activity, of letting thoughts come...and then letting them go. It is a focus of tuning in to our environment and tuning out the busy-ness of doing all the time. This is the place in nature where the outer landscape and our inner landscape entwine.

I believe that co-teacher of years ago was telling the children the worthwhileness of just being, of how immensely productive such inactivity in nature is for our souls. Still Sitting reminds me of how a natural flow can be so much more productive than the busiest of moments. There is a lot to learn from meditative quiet. From observation. From stillness in the out-of-doors.

Of Acorns and Oaks

I have a compulsion for gathering acorns— oval and polished like water worn stones, or greenish and round—they fill my pockets. Sometimes I collect just their scalloped brown caps. Back home I put them into jars for display, or for use in fairy house creations. The gathering urge is strong. I'm told it's biological. I'm told it's because I am a woman, and women have always been gatherers.

During my teenage Euell Gibbons days I gathered acorns from the white oak (*Quercus alba*), painstakingly cracked them open, picked out the little meats, and then soaked them in a stocking in the creek for several days. Once pulled out and dried, I ground the acorn nuts to make a fine meal to add to muffins. They had lost their tannic acids due to the heavy washing, but much of their sweetness as well.

As a child, Thanksgiving at my house always included a wooden tray of assorted nuts in their shells: cashews, walnuts, pecans, and

more—as well as two or three nutcrackers. We kids busied (
cracking and picking at the meats, a distraction while the adul
themselves in the kitchen, the aroma of sweet potatoes, turkey, gravy
and stuffing competing with the richness of the meats at hand. Acorns
were used only for decorating the Thanksgiving wreath.

Acorns can be consumed as is, but most are fairly bitter. Boiling
the nut meats in several changes of water and then roasting them,
with or without a sprinkle of sugar, creates a delicacy.

Ethnobotanists have observed that some areas of the Amazon
are so abundant with such a diversity of nut trees that they could
only have occurred through intentional planting. Such prehistoric
people planted trees as forage for future generations. Could our
abundance of oak, walnut, hickory and — once-upon-a-time,
chestnut— in the Finger Lakes, have something to do with
indigenous people of long ago? Were they planting food for their
children and grandchildren? Surely, these plantings were tailed after
by other lovers of nuts – the squirrels.

Squirrels bury acorns in little holes called caches, here and
there, throughout the fall for winter food supplies. Supposedly,
squirrels don't remember where they buried their nuts, no map is
made, no real markers left. Squirrels find their nuts, or another
squirrel's buried treasure, by means of smell. They smell the nut, or
even their own saliva they left upon it. I've read that a squirrel can
smell a buried acorn a mile off. I have not observed it myself, but it
would be fun to track.

Of course, oaks are pretty good at natural dispersal as well.

Acorns begin to drop in late August and continue ripening on the tree through December. Our main groups of oak in this area are the pointy, spine-tip lobed leaves of the red oak variety, which includes our common northern red oak, and the round lobed white oaks which also include the bur oak and the chestnut oak. Most of the chestnut oak I find are at the higher elevations along south-facing gorges like the one at the Wesley Hill Preserve in Honeoye. There are over 70 species of oaks just in North America, including a host of natural hybrids. Oaks, and our many other nut trees, are considered mast, or food, for wildlife like deer, bear, turkey, blue jays, squirrels and others.

Since ancient times the oak has been a symbol of courage, strength, and endurance, something its very wood is known for. Not surprisingly, the acorns themselves symbolize fertility.

While the deciduous leaves of the season now rest upon the ground, oaks carry theirs in a russet hue through the harshest months of winter. Oaks don't shed like most trees, they hold on to their dry, raspy leaves for months. This tendency is termed marcescence, which means delayed leaf dropping. Ecologists theorize a few reasons for this adaptation. It may be marcescence provides the large growing tree with natural pruning when branches, hung heavy with snow due to accumulation on remaining leaves, break from the weight. Or it may be more beneficial to drop leaves in the spring when the organic matter that accumulates is more usable to the tree and its seedlings. Delayed leaf dropping may also offer some frost protection for next spring's buds, or serve as a deterrent to browsing deer. Marcescence may just be an evolutionary delay; oaks were once evergreen, like the live oak species down south, and so possibly the oak tree is still in the process of developing deciduous tendencies from an evergreen ancestry. The oak is still becoming.

I have always loved gathering acorns, and have equally loved the russet and burgundy auburn colors of oak leaves, their rustling in the wind in late fall on into wintertime. I once used to wish I had hair the color of winter oak leaves and searched for such dyes. And then, if I could not have such hair, that I might one day have a lovely daughter with locks the color of winter oak leaves, one who would wander the woods with me to gather acorn caps and other small delights.

And I do.

evening
Primrose

The Remains of November

There is a simple grace to the elemental, stark feel of a November day that my spirit feels drawn to. The dark denim sky, tree branches stretched like dancer's arms, the somber color of fallen oak leaves scattered under low lighting beg me to answer solitude with solitude, to nestle in, to find rest. We've had snow twice this season up in the hills, once enough to stick and hang heavy in the trees. Then the weather warmed again into the 60s to call me back to the garden to dig the last of the purple heirloom carrots, pull what onions remained, and eat one forgotten squash after another.

Formations of geese passed and the last of the monarchs disappeared while hardy yellow sulfurs continued to flitter here and there. I always wait to hear the low wonk-wonk of snow geese traveling by night, but even they must have found southern territory by now. There is no season as lonely as November, when everyone has left by wing, or left inside the wrapping of cocoons and woody galls, or sent down deep into roots to slumber. The annuals leave only their skeletal forms: tiny dried vase-like calyxes of evening primrose, tall seed bearing stalks of mullein, and creamy seed heads of goldenrod. November is the pendulum point that stops a moment to pause, get its bearings, and swing on to the arc of winter.

All around are the remains of summer's memories, its fruitfulness, its sensual smells, drowsy hums and diminishing chirps. If I look closely I can remember summer still and take comfort in this passing. In the naked limbs of my most closely surrounding trees are now visible the nests of last summer's birds. Behind my bedroom is a robin's nest, built above the crook in the tree branch there and lined with grasses, and down in the woods a vireo nest is hung below the branch, just over three inches wide, and lined with fine fibers, pine needles, and spider silk.

Along the roadside, high and dangling from a black walnut tree, is a bald-faced hornet nest made from wood fiber and wasp saliva blended into a globe of small swirled patches that I never saw in summer. The bald-faced hornet is white and black on the posterior with a partially white face. The nest is begun in the spring by a pregnant female who makes a simple set of paper chambers and lays a few eggs to tend. The pupae that emerge are entirely worker females who take over their mother's duties so she can become "queen." It's not until fall that any male offspring are produced. Late fall's fertilized females find an old log to burrow into for the winter while the rest of the colony, including the queen, die. According to folklore, hanging a bald faced hornet nest in the house will dispel headaches. If you decide to collect one keep in mind that the empty nest often houses other insects and spiders seeking winter quarters.

Along these slips of land between the lakes and hills I begin to feel confined despite the opening of sky and the leafless season brings. The end of deer-bow season only makes me wary about wandering in the woods, not imprisoned by it. When rifle season starts my heart races, my ears go alert, and I sometimes duck on my own front porch. I run out into post-rifle season snow like a woman crazed for freedom to roam without dressing in blaze orange, not wanting to ruin someone else's hunt with my wandering.

In this barren season the human-land relationship grows strikingly evident; from the top of my driveway I count over 40 wind turbines spinning by day and blinking like Rudolph's nose by night. A huge orange glow rises up from the gas substation over the hill across Route 53. Both are constant reminders to me of our dependency on energy resources. But when I hear proponents of hydrofracking say that the method of extraction—high pressure fracturing deep underground while injecting a toxic chemical slurry of acetone, toluene, benzene, phenol, arsenic, barium, heavy metals and more to flush it out—as being sound science, I wonder what science they are talking about? Gas extraction and hydraulic fracturing science is, I suppose, a science, too, after all. But it's far too ghastly a danger to the environment and human health to be based on anything close to ecological or environmental science.

I often sigh and wonder why I had to be born in the fossil fuel era when there seems to be so little good to say about it. Like many here I want to live cooperatively with the land, with the earth and sun, the moon and stars, not as part of a society that will be remembered for blowing the earth to bits deep from within its core, slurping up all it has to give, then burning our drink into an atmospheric-climate-altering smog that comes back down as toxic rain (my environmental career began in acid rain science as a cloud collector on Whiteface Mountain). Surely an intelligent life forms like ourselves can find a better way to produce energy, one that doesn't risk our water, soil, climate and fellow creatures? I am thankful for these beautiful hills and Finger Lakes, for hot water, heat, and electricity (luxuries I have lived without elsewhere) but can we be truly thankful today if what we leave our children and grandchildren tomorrow is a land that resembles only the remains of November?

WINTER

Winter Solstice

It is solstice season and the sunrise has somersaulted slowly along the southern hilltop towards a halted journey on a narrower arc in the sky.

These days are now more dim than daylight.

Go out anyway.

In winter the world colors contrast with dualities of light and dark: black capped chickadees, slate colored juncos, stark branches against white-washed skies. Crows. When the occasional cardinal comes he appears lit like flames of crimson. The jay boasts blue.

It's a season of turning inward, a season of sleep, dreaming, and recovery. The turtles are huddled in muddy banks, snakes below ground curl in knots, and even white-footed mice and voles of different kinds may nest together for warmth. It is the season of the caw of fan-tailed crows, who know their name, and the rattle of ravens, who do not care.

Go out anyway.

A slumbering porcupine may slip from the treetops and tumble toward ground, as they sometimes do, but to worry about being hit by quills while out in the woods does us no good.

Go out anyway.

Somewhere in a hole below, a chipmunk is tucked tight with its tail, a cache of shagbark hickory nuts and acorns nearby, while he waits out winter's chill. The black bear, for whose dens I scout in summer's glorious green days, sleeps more soundly. I am more likely to stumble upon one in deep snow beneath the stump of a tree than in some hidden hollow.

I go there still.

There is light in this season, be it the stars and snow crystals above or below: a seed tucked in tight and waiting, the peeper's call (a silenced bell waiting to be rung). Be it the steps of a whitetail deer, or the whinny of the screech owl strung from branch to branch. There are lights that adorn the darkness, both outside and within ourselves.

Go out and glow with it all. The world catches fire from such happenings.

White throated Sparrow

Feathers, Snow, and Sorrow

"Those who dwell among the beauties and mysteries of the earth are never alone or weary of life." -Rachel Carson

I.

Nature is a constant reminder that there is a spirit of life that exists beyond the doings of man. It's not difficult to connect with that spirit, and even if you can't get outdoors, there are always the birds. A winter feeder or two, with plenty of black oil sunflower seeds, a suet block—even peanut butter on stale bread—will bring them close. The birds at my feeders are dressed much like winter businesspeople in dark grays, black, tan, and just a hint or russet or daring red here or there. I had an evening grosbeak at the feeder in November, bringing back memories of my Vermont days watching the birds at the feeder with my baby boy on my hip. This winter I have a colorful pair of cardinals, at least two tribes of chick-a-dees, white and red breasted nuthatch mascots, swarms of dark-eyed juncos (actually in the sparrow family), kingly looking blue jays (of course), downy and hairy woodpeckers, pine siskin, and a couple tree sparrows. I was surprised to see this harbinger of spring, the tree sparrow, and thought at first it must have been a chipping sparrow with its ruddy crown, but no, there was the dark "stick pin" in the center of its pale chest.

The winter may bring a host of unexpected visitors: major birding sights are predicting the appearance of crossbills, evening grosbeaks, and pine grosbeaks in our area. Recently, a birder up at Durand Eastman Park in Rochester documented a Type 3 red crossbill (there are several types evolving new adaptations right now, Type 3 has the smallest bill). White-winged crossbills, red crossbills, and the grosbeaks are erupting in new regions like ours this season— some traveling across the entire U.S. due to spruce and hemlock seed declines in the Northwest states and Canada. Other less-frequently sighted species, like bohemian waxwings, will be here looking for buckthorn berries and other wild fruits, due to years of heavy drought throughout the north and central Midwest. Most will then leave, heading north to search out nutritious boreal mountain ash berries to sustain themselves on.

Rarely seen birds, with their unexpected colorings and element of surprise, are like soul food for the eyes. There will be other winged wonders to spot, flocks of snow buntings will arrive and there are whisperings about the potential of boreal owls wintering here this year as well.

II.

I cannot imagine a world without snow. Last week, at Winter Solstice time, while the valley below waited for a few degrees more of a drop, you could drive up just a couple of miles from Naples, NY, and enter a small snow line of white-etched trees and frosted ground. The feeling was magical. Winter in sepia tones that blend into gloomy skies and long nights are simply too stark and barren without the land light of snow.

I cannot imagine a world without snow because the shadows of winter are such long ones. We are forced to be stiller than were before, to venture inward both more physically (in our homes and more psychologically. Since time began, northern peoples have drummed to ward off the dark spirits of the season, huddled close for warmth and comfort, lit fires and called their shamans and storytellers to join them. Many early peoples and far north native traditions did not see a clear delineation between the metaphysical world and the physical one; they could communicate with wild animals, with their ancestors, with spirits, and with the earth. I think that winter reminds us of these lost connections and our need for them now more than any other time of the year.

I cannot imagine a world without the light of snow, a landscape drenched in heavy silence, an earth and sky decorated in crystalline structures of all kinds. Snow is purifying. Snow covers a world in its cycle of death and passing and sleep with something physically miraculous, the light of which is like an inner flame. Environmentally, snow is also a source for recharging our springs, wells, and lakes. It is prelude to a summer of precious water and also a source to recharge ourselves, to offer play, diversion, and respite, giving us a whole new dimension to our world and our lives. I cannot imagine my home's winter landscape without snow.

III.

I cannot imagine a world without hope just as I cannot imagine a world without snow or birds. Kathleen Dean Moore writes in the introduction to her book, *Wild Comfort,* "I don't know what despair is, if it's something or nothing, a kind of filling up or an emptying out. I don't know what sorrow does to the world, what it adds or takes away." But she adds later: "How we feel about events, how we respond to them, how we transform them and judge them – these are our own decisions...a matter of the shape of our spirit, the corrugation of the feathers in our wings." We can learn a lot from the birds; recall the wonder of their hollow bones, their feather structure, their breaking down of territories in winter's season to be in community. For sorrow's sake I will do only what I can: try to feel the cleansing of freshly fallen snow, watch the birds, fold paper and cut intricate snowflake forms, again and again, to send love to the families of children in sorrow shared, honor those who have lost their loved ones, and work to be part and witness to the world shining on.

(composed shortly after yet another school massacre, this at Sandy Hook Elementary School, CT, 2012)

Stars in a Winter Sky

How is it that the sky feeds the stars?

— Lucretius, 54 BCE

Driving up and over the High Road the other evening my daughter commented how she loved driving at night this time of year because it looked like we were traveling through outer space. As I looked out at the stars in the sky, with mankind's lights along the hillsides below, the stars above, and both forms of lighting reflected in Canandaigua Lake, I could see her point—it was as if we were completely surrounded by starlight from above and below. My jeep had become her spaceship. But what is a star, really? Stars are amazing energy burners, consuming all that they are; dense masses of hydrogen gas fuel destined to eventually use up their resources, to age and dim, or age and explode. The physics of it all is quite complex and not something I would venture to describe.

A star takes a very, very long time to form. The gravitational collapse of the swirling gases, what is called a protostar, can take some 100,000 years to form. After that, it's just brief million more years before nuclear fusion occurs and the star is born. Stars, depending on their type, can live for trillions or billions of years before burning out, and there are countless billions of them in the universe.

Stars come in many different sizes, or densities as it were, and based on their rate of burning, will turn into older Red Giant, Blue Giant or Super Red Giants before going Supernova and exploding with unfathomable power or, on the opposite end of the spectrum, take the quieter forms of white dwarves, neutron stars, or black holes.

I don't know much about stars, but like most people, I know our brightest magnitude star in the Northern Hemisphere is Polaris, on the tip of the Little Dipper's handle. Polaris is our current pole star, only one degree from the Northern Celestial Pole and still getting closer. Because the earth wobbles a bit on its axis (a term called "the procession of equinoxes") Polaris will not be and has not always been the true North Star. 5,000 years ago, during the time of the Egyptians, the North Star was Thuban, in the constellation Draco.

A favorite winter constellation is Orion, the Hunter, who rules the winter sky. This is one of the most ancient of constellations in our circumpolar group and can been seen now in the south-central sky as a huge rectangle of four stars with a three-starred belt. Orion's right shoulder is the star Betelgeuse, a Red Giant near the end of its life. His left foot is the blue star, Regal, thought to be both nearly done fusing its heavy elements and beginning to collapse into itself in a supernova, or about to dim into a White Giant. Ancient Greeks saw Orion the Hunter with his arm raised and holding a club to fight off Taurus the Bull (look for the V-shape of the bull's horns just above Orion). Orion is gallant and fights Taurus, The Bull, to protect The Pleiades—a small cluster of stars known in Greek mythology as the Seven Sisters.

North American indigenous people on this continent had their own interpretations of the night sky. To some southern tribes, Polaris was a mountain goat who climbed too high up the precipice of a mountain and became stuck. Great Spirit took the brave goat to live with him in the heavens. In other North American legends, The Pleiades were seen as seven adventurous brothers with one little sister. The Big Dipper was The Great Fisher, and the belt and sword of Orion were two canoes racing for a prized salmon, never to be caught, that sent the seasons from winter to summer and back again. Others looked to the night sky and interpreted each star as the possible campfire of ancestors who watched over them, waiting to guide them home.

More modern interpretations of our relationship to the stars include professor and author, Gerald Grow, who writes, "You and I are not merely separated from the galaxies by unimaginable immensities of space; we are also connected to them by unimaginable immensities of time. We are literally made from stars. We are their descendants. The only difference between us and stars is time." Renowned astrophysicist and astronomer, Carl Sagan, said it more simply - "we are star-stuff."

Looking to the stars we can see our connection to everything on the planet and beyond. The oxygen we breathe was created from the stuff of Earth, the stuff of Earth was created from the stuff of stars, the stuff of stars and space was created from one tiny point that inflated to an enormous size over a dozen billions years to form the cosmos in a process known as the Big Bang. All the elemental stuff of life and stars has always been and will always be. We are connected to one another, to life, to the universe, through matter and time. In the words of the notorious, most notably spaced-out musician, Jerry Garcia, "We're the same stuff as stars and galaxies, so we're indivisibly part of it. We're the part that speaks, that plays music, that creates abstractions."

I don't know enough about stars but seeing them reminds me of one important thing: no matter what we do, and no matter who we are, what religion we practice, or the many ways in which we think, the stars remind me that each and every one of us is connected to something far greater then ourselves.

Coyote

Adapting to Winter

Looking out the window on a chilly winter day makes me realize how amazingly hardy species other than myself truly are. Northern species have three choices regarding how to deal with winter: migrate, adapt or die. Here in our temperate climate winter means life or death; death being a very good option for some organisms where fecundity of the species is the primary goal. For many animals and insects, from the Canada goose to the green darner dragonfly, migrating south is a wonderful adaptation. But those species that plan to stay put for winter must harden to it.

Trees, who provide heat for me in winter, cannot produce their own internal heat. They must adapt to winter's freeze through a hardening process that is more complicated than merely dropping leaves. During the first stage of hardening, water within the plant cells moves outside the cell so frozen ice crystals cannot damage the delicate intracellular structures. The cytoplasm (intracellular fluid) is replaced with a chemical brew that is like a concentrated antifreeze.

If a warm spell, or false spring occurs, the chemicals begin to convert back to cellular water. When a following cold snap refreezes, the intracellular water will cause the tree popping sounds often heard in the woods on very cold days. These pops can severely crack and even destroy a tree. Our maples and oaks usually withstand freezing temperatures down to -30 degrees F. In boreal areas, hardening reaches a third stage where certain trees, like white spruce, handle temperatures down to an amazing -80 degrees F without damage.

Not all plants are totally dormant in wintertime. Evergreen plants like Christmas stocking fern and lycopodium, some algae, and even the greenish-grey bark of poplar trees can conduct small amounts of photosynthesis in winter. The deficit loss of energy to do so is usually greater than the energy produced, so our pines and spruces remain primarily in a state of inactivity all winter long.

A similar hardening event occurs in insects and amphibians that enter torpidity: a type of hibernation similar to suspended animation. Animals like spring peeper frogs and stonefly larvae use cryoprotection so the piercing crystallization of water molecules cannot destroy the living cells in their bodies. In spring peepers, cellular water is replaced with a high sugar antifreeze that won't change back until temperatures thaw out well above freezing. The only true mammal hibernators we have in the area are jumping mice and little brown bats, the latter of which are in severe decline because of a fungal disease rampant in most hibernacula.

Black bears lower their respiration rate and heartbeats to barely detectable levels, but on warm winter days they may rouse to look for food. A pregnant female (a sow) will give birth while sleeping. Her preemie-like newborns weigh roughly ¾ of a pound. Baby cubs are introduced to the world in the height of our coldest season, burrowing into their mother's warm fur and nursing to survive. By spring they've gained nearly six pounds off their slumbering mama's milk before emerging. Is it no wonder that the bear is often symbolized as womb of the earth?

Mammals like chipmunks and skunks enter long periods of sleeping through winter without truly hibernating; and winter birds like the chick-a-dee enter a torpid state, similar to a mini-hibernation, to survive extremely cold nights.

Being hardy enough for this landscape takes on a new light when I think about how truly well-adapted some forms of life are for this region, as I myself put another log into the woodstove and boil water for my tea. I am thankful for my own abilities to keep warm, aside from having enough food and warm clothes, I can shovel snow to rev my internal engine heat. We all have our own ways of hardening up for the season, be it canning vegetables from the garden, splitting and stacking wood, layering on the long johns, or waxing the cross-country skis. We humans have no true physiological adaptations to cold; we are delicate in comparison to other northern species who survive winter, yet we too are hardy in our ability to create unique adaptations all our own.

A Legend Among Wildlife

There is a phantom in the woods. I see signs of him everywhere. The five-toed tracks are rather large, 2 ½ inches across, with retractable crescent claws. I find their tracks bounding through the hemlock glens and meandering across the top of Bristol Mountain. Their tracks make me think of a little bear. This animal, said to be active both night and day, eludes me.

I saw one once. In the Adirondacks. It was while I was working as a cloud collector on Whiteface Mountain. My brain registered large black cat, before my mind's cataloging process scrolled down to fisher, one of the largest members of the weasel family. Having once been extirpated from New York State, there are now trapping seasons for fisher in some areas of even the Central and Southern Tier regions. When I hear of local cougar sightings, I often think of how a fisher might appear like that from a distance— a black panther of sorts.

The Anishinabe and Algonquin Native Americans called fisher, Gitchi Odjig, Great Fisher. He was considered an adopted brother to the in-between god and hero known as Nanabozho. Great Fisher was known for his bravery and magical powers, but mostly as the one who released the birds of summer in Skyland so that we would not have endless winter, but four seasons instead. For this brave contribution, Great Spirit hung fisher in the night sky in what we know as The Great Dipper, or Ursa Major. I never could see the bear in that arrangement of stars; the long handle makes more sense as the long fluffy tail of a fisher.

Maybe I spend too much time looking down instead of up. A female fisher will den up in the treetops to raise her nest of 2-3 kits. She can also turn her hind feet nearly 180 degrees so that coming down a trunk is conducted as easily as a squirrel might do. The resilient fisher is an opportunistic feeder who eats an omnivorous selection of acorns, beechnuts, berries, and apples along with rabbits, squirrels, grouse, mice, shrews and carrion. A deer carcass is a feast that fisher will take up residence near until there are only bones and hair left to pick from its teeth. But it is the fierceness of fisher that stands out most. Fisher is the only hunter of porcupines, attacking from the front until the quilled animal is weakened, or knocking them out of the tree tops, wasting nothing but a hide of quills in the end.

Last year my friend had two fisher in his backyard, raising quite the cat-style ruckus, so much so that at first he thought they might have been cats. Six years ago, two teens in Naples were surprised to find a fisher in their trap along Naples Creek close to the village. The animal was released from the leg hold, and reported. I can only imagine how brave the children must have been as well, to be so close to an animal all sharp teeth and snarls, an animal driven by an endless will to hunt, and not be seen. What it is like to find an animal you weren't looking for, and didn't know was even a resident in the area? (Since that time, I too have come upon a fisher at last, when my dog treed it. I can tell you first hand it didn't seem afraid, but snarled and chattered, scurrying up and down the tree at us).

As our forest ecosystems in the Finger Lakes continue to regenerate and mature, so too do the hidden habitats they provide. But species that make a comeback must still adapt to things not-quite-as-they-once-were. They must adapt to fragmented woods, climate change, and other human activity. That animals like black bears, bald eagles, and fishers can once again reside here is a testament to environmental recovery, but these and other species will need to continue to adapt to our changing world. I keep eyes on their tracks, searching for a glimpse of the fierce and legendary fishers, who probably know my whereabouts more than I do theirs.

What tracks do we humans leave behind? More than the obvious roads and buildings, wind turbines and jet trails in the sky, more than our trappings and waste. What prints do we scatter into the natural places with our hunting, our recreation, our breaths or even our minds? We go to the wilder places to let go of some of the modernity in our lives or to reunite with our connection to the earth. Surely we leave these tracks of intention there as well, as yearnings to remember the trails from whence we came, and to remember the origins of our very nature.

Just the other side of Groundhog's Day

Whether the climate be changin'
Or whether the weather's temperature climbs
Even if you think global warmin's just a theory
It'll still take some evolvin' to survive.

Snow fleas. I've spotted more specs of them all through this winter than I can ever recall seeing in all my life. They emerge from the soil and leaf litter around tree wells, or in other high albedo spots, and pepper the supranivean surface in numbers akin to stars in the sky. Don't panic, these miniscule creatures aren't fleas at all, but primitive, wingless arthropods *(Hypogastrura nivicola)* known more commonly as springtails. Snow fleas come out on late, warm winter days to feed on snow algae, lichens, spores and leaf molds. They can be found worldwide, from the Arctic to the Antarctic. Of course, to prove that their multitudes are early and burgeoning more

164

this year than ever before, I would have to set up some sort of scientific experiment: transects and a system for counting the lively little blue-black specs, have some baseline data, and record the results over many winters. They would take time to count as it would be similar to counting grains of sand.

One of the best interpretive costumes I ever saw was a man dressed up in a life-size springtail/snow flea outfit, hand-sewed by his wife. The costume was complete with six arms as well as the special appendage on its fourth abdominal segment—a furcular—being the spring-like organ it uses to propel itself. With six arms dangling, the assuming fellow talked about springtails while fidgeting and flailing his oversized furcula to the hysterics of a blushing audience. In real life, snow fleas are less than 6 mm long. They are small, numerous, ancient, and highly successful.

Insects have many ways of dealing with winter's freeze. Some lay eggs and die, some migrate, many others go into a state of diapause or hibernation. Even with the varied adaptations insects have to withstand winter's chill, a vast number of winter hardy insects succumb to especially harsh weather. It's almost like a pruning of sorts. But when warm winters occur we have more insects surviving until spring, and more insects available to reproduce the following year.

According to the National Oceanographic Atmospheric Administration (NOAA), 2016 was the warmest year on record, followed only by 2015 and 2017. The trend ranks 2018 only slightly behind as the fourth hottest year in 138 years. Each passing year is one also of major droughts and record forest fires. The forest fires out West were blamed partially on increased insect damage creating moribund trees, as well declining snowpack in the higher elevations.

Last week, my groundhog refused to come out (he is, after all, a true hibernator). But if he had, I bet he'd predict another warmer-than-average year.

Sometimes I wonder if our grandchildren will know what a snow-filled winter looks like, wonder if they might miss the magic of the crystalline white world, the gliding along under snow-laden branches on skis, building a snowman, and shoveling. Yes, that too. Some might not mind the idea of such a loss, thinking that snow enthusiasts can just travel to higher elevations to enjoy the cold fluff. It is doubtful that winter and snow will disappear entirely, but the fickle comings and goings of our winter season is like a planet with bipolar disorder.

Sudden Stratospheric Warming (SSW) can cause oscillating temperatures from super warm to severely frigid in winter. In the atmospheric layer cake above us—the troposphere, stratosphere and mesosphere—a sudden warming can be caused in part by a complex land-ocean temperature variations. A warm layer descends into the circumpolar vortex and switches the typical winter westerly air flow into an unusual easterly. Visually, the jet stream in the Arctic buckles and sort of pulsates downward, blasting places like Great Britain and South Carolina with really cold air. Here in Upstate New York, we're back to real winter.

Weather is a fickle thing. What's needed to resolve the phenomena of SSW is, believe it or not, a sort of earthly exhale into outer space. Triggers for weather changes like Stratospheric Warming can range from thermal dynamics to sunspot activity. But unlike weather, climate is usually something you can count on. The National Climate Assessment, and many scientists, tell us that the extreme weather events we see now are what climate change looks like. A 2011 report from the International Energy Agency also report that we only have a few years to take major action reducing our fossil fuel emissions, and other greenhouse gases, if anything can be done to change our present trajectory as a hot planet. I think about snow fleas, and how, to these soil creatures, the planet above might seem to be the entire universe itself and how maybe, to such little lives so primitive and small, we are like slipshod gods running the show.

Stellar Crystal or Dendrite

Snow

Snow the struggle. Snow the muse. Most of us have heard that the Inuit have over forty names for snow. We have a few; there's the kid version of "yahoo, snow!" and the adult version of "*!@# snow!" Skiers, snowboarders, and other snow enthusiasts like myself may have a few more like: powder snow, corn snow, and packed powder. But there is a world of snow terminology reflective of the complexity of snow crystal formation and its subsequent ever-changing landscape that leaves me breathless.

Outside my window today the tree branches are outlined in white lace. Quali is the Inuit name for snow collecting on branches, and is a term used by scientists today. Typically, it's not just any snow that collects this way and if I take a hand lens to a snow laden branch, I am stunned by the sight of thousands of stellar dendrite crystals; branched or fern-like ornaments each created from one single droplet of water that fell in grace and movement thousands of feet up from here.

All snowflake crystal structures begin with a tiny droplet of water nucleating around a dust particle and freezing into a hexagonal prism. The resulting nano scale prism, shaped like anything from a thin plate to a pencil stub, begins to develop facets and arms on a six-sided structure that all emerge simultaneously, and accordingly, in different cloud temperatures and wind conditions on the way down to earth. The amount of moisture in the air, the temperature at each heavenly stratification, and the wind, all combine to determine the type of crystal that will form into what we call collectively— snow.

The amazing possibilities of geometric forms the initial crystal prism may morph into are truly astounding; from highly geometric capped columns to fantasia like radiating dendrites, from triangular crystals to twelve-sided stars. Given the same conditions all crystals will grow in basically the same way. For example, needle snow is formed around 23 degrees. Nature designs the pattern that will emerge given the right set of circumstances, like in the division of cells, only crystals aren't actually alive. According to Caltech physicist, snowflake author, and photographer, Kenneth Libbrecht, "there is no blueprint or genetic code that guides the growth of a snowflake, yet marvelously complex structures appear, quite literally out of thin air."

The snow created at Bristol Mountain and Hunt Hollow by snow machines, much as I appreciate it, has no crystal form. But that doesn't mean humans can't reproduce crystal structure. The study of crystal formation is important to our technological advances for computers, energy, and more.

The magic of snow doesn't end when it hits the ground; snow on the ground metamorphoses in various ways. Once snow crystals become part of terra firma they develop plasticity and exhibit many of the same similarities as tar. Snow also absorbs heat and radiates sunlight-two reasons why a snow shelter is always warmer than the air temperature outside and why sunscreen is a good idea if you're heading out to the slopes for the day.

Wildlife depends on snow during the winter months both for insulation and for protection from predators. The subnivean world (that area within and beneath the cover of snow) offers protective space for mice and voles to tunnel into that help hide them from hawks and owls, although not from the keen sense of smells of fox and coyotes. Rain and freezing that create snowscapes glazed over in ice are a problem for critters accustomed to moving with ease within the snowpack but provide easier travel for those who walk on top. Snowpack also provides a sledding surface for mink and otters. After all, people aren't the only ones who enjoy the snow.

From each single brilliant frozen crystalline gem a new world is created each year, with each storm or a gentle flurry. Henry David Thoreau said it best when he wrote, "I should hardly admire more if real stars fell and lodged on my coat. Nature is full of genius, full of the divinity, so that not a snowflake escapes its fashioning hand."

Natural Elevation

The other morning, after a snowfall with a grey sky that whispered of more squalls to come, I noticed a purple finch sitting on top of my jeep's passenger side door. There was a break in the clouds and he seemed to be sunning himself. A gust of wind blew in and he did something I've never observed before: he leapt off the car and "surfed" the wind alongside the car window, and then lifted and landed atop the car again when the breeze subsided. Did I really just witness a bird playing with the wind? A moment later another gust came in, and again, the bird dipped down off the car and appeared to surf, wings out but not moving, until the gust stopped and he rose to the rooftop again, looking keenly in the direction of the wind as if anticipating another wave.

I laughed in surprise at the playfulness of this wild bird.

Winter is full of crystalline beauty, peace—and the opportunity for enjoyment. Taking time to get out into Nature in all seasons is beneficial to our bodies, our minds, and our spirits too. Fresh air and sunshine reduces our susceptibility to colds and flu, as well as depression and anxiety. Studies show that time outdoors, and unplugged, decreases stress and eases the mind while increasing our creativity and sense of well-being. Adding the component of outdoor play to our lives is the most natural way to elevate mood.

The ways in which we move through the winter world have another deep effect on us. Hiking over frozen ground and through snow is a worthwhile workout, but winter urges us to glide silently—to skate and ski and sled—or glide more noisily via snowmobile as well. There is a special joy that comes from playing with the true nature of snow that we knew intuitively as children. We can reclaim that naturally elevated feeling when we find the glide again as adults.

Dr. John Kitchen, a retired neurologist who now goes by the name, Slomo, has dedicated his remaining years to gliding up and down the boardwalks of San Diego on roller blades. He refers to the effect of lateral motion on the brain as *the zone*—something like pure bliss. Anyone who enjoys time on skis, or sledding down a hill, can probably relate to these good vibrations.

Many of our recent winters have been a little tough for finding enough fluffy stuff, but around here we are blessed with high elevation drumlins (elongated hills of glacial sediments) that often have snow up top when the folks in the valley have none. Harriet Hollister Spencer State Recreation Area, with an elevation over 2,000 feet, catches some of the lake effect snows off Lake Erie over Western New York. I've often driven down Canadice Road in Springwater to just a half mile from the entrance before seeing any snow, getting there to find a mystical Narnia winter awaiting. Harriett's micro-climate makes it a great place for cross country, skate skiing, winter mountain biking, snowmobiling, and hiking.

Ontario County Park, with an elevation of 2,256 feet, is another snowy high point in the region. There are trails near the exit of the park that are especially for cross country skiing. Some of the trails run into miles of the Finger Lakes Trail Bristol Branch as well, so download a map before heading out. Open areas on the hilltop offer potential for sledding.

Cumming Nature Center in Naples is another high elevation, at 1,745 ft., so there is seasonally more snow there than in the valleys. Best of all, the 900 acre nature center has over 15 miles of trails through some of the most beautiful skiing – or hiking – around. You can find the tracks of mink, otter, coyotes, and more in the quiet of these wild woodland trails. And the Nature Center itself offers all the amenities including a fireplace and an eating area where you can bring your own crockpots, bird feeding stations outside the windows, exhibits, and FREE popcorn! A true Nordic skier's paradise.

Bristol Mountain Nordic Ski Center is located at about 2,200 feet at the summit of Bristol Mt. So many a winter season the man-made snow up top is the only place to go for cross country skiing, aside from driving north to the Tug Hill Plateau in the southern Adirondacks. There is sad irony in the fact that snowmaking uses energy that contributes to global warming, and global warming, in turn, reduces our chances for snow.

Cross country skiing is the way I fell in love with winter and the joy of snow. I taught my children how to ski Nordic and alpine, and almost learned to snowboard, but after watching how painful it was when my son began, I chickened out. I telemark ski downhill, and I teach both types of Nordic skiing, classic and skate, the latter of which I think feels a lot like flying, or maybe a bird surfing in the wind.

A Flurry Out Of Time

I.

I was carpooling with a friend to work when she said she had a treat for me. She pulled out an old cloth-bound copy of naturalist and philosopher, John Burroughs, *Winter Sunshine*, and began to read. Burroughs' musings on the winter landscape, his wisdom and stunning imagery filled the car with the scent of fresh wood chips from a frosty ax, the quiet of snow, the meaning behind the passing tracks of a red fox. I thought how much I, too, love winter; this winter, a real winter. I thought how inspiring the thoughtful pace of Burroughs' wanderings were compared to how much like weasels we are, running from one curiosity and task to another, hardly stopping at all, making a flurry out of time.

II.

My daughter is standing by the door, her fake fur hat framing her face, wearing Sorrel boots, a snowsuit and mitts. I think how cozy and perfect for the season she looks when she takes me by surprise and scrunches up her face whining, "I hate New York!" I know that what she really means is that she hates winter. My youngest child, the one I raised skiing on my back before she could walk, then taught to ski on her own as soon as she could walk; the daughter who sledded and built snow dragons; the one who studied whales in northern seas in British Columbia and in New Brunswick, dreams of Florida even though she has never been there ever in her life. She wants to go to college in Florida next year—which does seem fitting for one whose passion is to be a marine biologist and save the oceans. But she also wants eternal summer. And, understandably, an ocean she can explore year-round.

III.

I don't want my daughter to go so far away. This cycle of growth and change, this separation of cells from my own body that has been happening for so many years still alarms me. If she goes so far away, then how many pennies a day will I have to save to afford airfare to bring me to her, or her to here? Doesn't she realize she will being giving up more than winter? Seasons like this are full of mystery and quiet; their seeds safely tucked in fists and pockets. Other seasons unfurl with wildness and yearning, or burst into fruit only to pause later. Seasons whir by and time is, again, a flurry. My daughter will not just be giving up a season, but moving on into another all her own. I love winter and snow. I am never the one eager to see winter end, but seasons change. I must let go of a season as well.

IV.

Lavender-hued blackberry canes bend to a winter landscape of greys and browns against white. The winter wind skitters across the pasture creating whirlwinds of snow that rise like crystalline spirits into the ethers. Scattered through the fields, winter weeds take on a beauty of their own: Queen Ann's Lace are empty nests of tiny stars, the primrose hold on to weathered woody vases full of next season's dreams while tall winter goldenrods nod their heads like hags whose hair is adorned with intricate flakes or downy feather. Winter is more than a season, it is a song of reflection from somewhere deep inside us. Winter is a rhythm of time in our bones. A light within our bellies. A place of muffled silence from whence imagination roars.

FOR ALL SEASONS

Seasons are ever-changing. Try spending time outdoors each day for a year, just watching and not doing anything, and tell me if you don't notice subtle shifts in the angle of sunlight and the lengthening of shadows long before summer wanes. Listen past the hum of humanity's movements and the buzz of technology. Discover for yourself the hatchings, bloomings, flockings, and migrations as they occur, each in its own time. By tuning into the cycles of the seasons and living things, by connecting to nature, we become witness to what may be changing forever. Developing an intimate relationship with the natural world is the foundation of stewardship.

Life teems with change. Crickets orchestrate the night for a short while, but as the earth tilts, chirping gives way to a silent song of starlight. A white oak sapling puts on a thin new layer of fresh growth rings each year, and over time becomes a shade tree. The oak, in turn, eventually becomes moribund and is decayed back into the earth by fungi, insects, and bacteria. The scope of changes like epochs, extinctions, adaptations, and evolution occur on a lengthy time scale compared to our brief lives. Yet the man-made changes to life on this planet, in a sliver of earth time, over the briefer era of just a few human generations, are accelerating. Such events need our attention.

Nature is a master of change and resurrection. Nature will endure. The real question may be whether or not humankind will endure. We need nature...but does nature need us? We are the ones who must determine how we will change to manage our impact on the earth and our climate. There are a multitude of solutions that include everything from reducing food waste and caring for our soil, to restructuring our energy grid to becoming more sustainable for ourselves and our planet.

We all change. I am not the same person I was a decade ago, or even last year. I would love to mark the passing of days by the waxing and waning moon; the passing of seasons by the budding of bloodroot, the glow of goldenrod, the smells of autumn, and the solace of winter. I would love to get my news from the creek that murmurs stories from whence it came, while gleefully pondering their going. But in this increasingly complex world, life—and all its changes—requires more attention than listening to the whispers of creeks. Such a world requires that we embrace nature's ability to adapt and that we welcome a season of spring-like, ever-emerging, ways of being. Each of us must prepare ourselves, and future generations, for these coming seasons of change so that our children may continue to find joy in watching bald eagles fish in shimmering lakes, in picking ripe fruit from fertile land, or simply gazing at the wonder of it all.

END NOTES

The Deep Under-The-Green

The quotation by Sandra Steingraber on page 10 is from "A Poem for the Marcellus." *Huffpost.com*. 02 May 2012. Web.

The Songs of Birds

In Spring Bird Song, the epigraph by Emily Dickinson is the first few lines from her poem, "The Saddest Noise, The Sweetest Noise." Her poem can be read in entirety at peotryverse.com

Creek Walking

The quote used from Henry David Thoreau is from his Journal dated 19-Aug 1851. Torrey, Bradford and Francis Allen, ed. *The Journal of Henry David Thoreau. 19-Aug 1851.* Boston: Houghton Mifflin, 1906.

Forget The Big Bad Wolf

The quote from Stephen Buhner is from his book, *Healing Lyme.* 2nd Edition. White River Junction: Raven Press; Chelsea Green Publishing, 2015. Print. p. 92.

Feathers, Snow, and Sorrow

The epigraph comes from Rachel Carson and was pulled from Rachel Carson Quotes. (n.d.). allauthor.com.

The quote from Kathleen Moore on page 107 is from her book, *Wild Comfort; The Solace of Nature.* "A Joke My Father Used to Tell." Trumpeter Books; Boston. 2010. p 82.

Stars in a Winter Sky

The epigraph is from Lucretius, 54 BCE and was found on the *WWU Physics/Astronomy Dept Page,* Updated 04/20/2019. Copyright 2019. Western Washington University. Web. The origin of this quote is from *De Rerum Naturam.*

The quote on page 110 by Gerald Grow is from his website blog, "We Are Literally Made From the Stars." *Gerald Grow's Website.* http://www.longleaf.net/ggrow/Stars.html. 1997. Web. Accessed 2015.

Snow

The Snowcrystals.com site that Kenneth Libbrecht manages includes scientific information and links to Libbrecht's spectacular photographic books for children and adults on snow crystals. It can be found at http://www.its.caltech.edu/~atomic/snowcrystals/faqs/faqs.htm.

The famous quotation about snow from Thoreau was accessed via the web and cited from as *Henry David Thoreau's Journal.* January 5, 1856.

ACKNOWLEDGEMENTS

Much appreciation is given to the hardworking newspaper editors who printed my past decade of nature columns, many of which appear in this book in slightly modified form. These publications include the former *Naples Record* (Ed. Amy Vangellow), *The Neapolitan* (Ed. Kim Torpey), *Lake Country Weekender* (Ed. Diane Olson), and *Owl Light News* (Ed. D.E. Bentley).

Immense gratitude to Kim Torpey for all her support and tireless effort helping design the cover for this book.

I would like to thank the following individuals who gave thoughtful and professional feedback during the developing stages of this manuscript: Sarah Blank (the amazing and always gracious coordinator at FLCC's The Write Place), Nick Aiezza (poet and assistant to the vice president of the president of The Write Place), George Payne (former chief philosopher and political writer at The Write Place), Nani Nehring-Bliss (former interim Director of The Write Place, because I am certain you also reviewed many early drafts of some of these essays) and to Dan Foltz (author and willing victim of my request).

Special thanks to Edward Hower for his meticulous attention to the details, and to Alison Lurie, author and Cornell professor emerita, for selecting my manuscript for the Cayuga Lake Book 2019 Creative Prose Award and publication. I am deeply honored.

I would also like to acknowledge all the mentors, named and unnamed, in this book. These essays are the results of learning and growth about our natural world, and our place within it, that you all have helped show me. To all of my teachers, I am so grateful.

Additional gratitude to my children, Skyler and Maeya, who have somehow lived through my attempts at homesteading and incessant delving into feral places. And to dear friends, especially, Jen Cervantes and Donna Starr, for helping me wield all these sometimes muddy, sometimes sunny, but ever-so-wondrous years.

ABOUT THE AUTHOR

Growing up on the wetlands of Irondequoit Bay, Angela Cannon-Crothers came to the Finger Lakes Region twenty years ago to raise a family after a decade of travel. Her passion for wild places and conservation had led her to work three seasons as a cloud collector on Whiteface Mountain in an acid rain study, as a fishing hand on a halibut boat off the coast of Alaska, a botany assistant on a glacier, a wilderness ranger and naturalist for the U.S. Forest Service, a trip guide, a horse wrangler/cook, and as an environmental educator at centers from Minnesota to New Hampshire. While homesteading back in New York, she worked as an instructor of Environmental and Soil Sciences at Finger Lakes Community College.

An avid writer, her articles, nature columns, and fiction have appeared in numerous magazines and literary journals. Her previous books include a novel, *The Wildcrafter*, a chapter in the anthology, *A Mile In Her Boots; Women Who Work in the Wild*, a creative nonfiction book, *Our Voices, Our Wisdom; An Herb Haven Year*, and a children's book, *Grape Pie Season*, illustrated by Darryl Abraham. Her previous awards include Finalist in nonfiction with the A Room Of Her Own Foundation, and Teacher Of Young People with Writers & Books in Rochester. And once, very long ago now, she received the Rochester Junior Literary Award for poetry with a poem about a field guide called, "Wildflowers of North America".

Now working at the Rochester Museum and Science Center's Cumming Nature Center, she resides in Naples with a Morgan-cross pony, two cats, a frog, and a dog named Moonshadow.

ABOUT CAYUGA LAKE BOOKS

The Cayuga Lake Books imprint was founded in 2012 by some authors from the Ithaca, New York, area who were looking for alternatives to mainstream publishing.

The goal of CLB is to find and encourage talented, original writers. Submissions are competitive. The four editors consider all manuscripts; we must all read and unanimously accept a work before we include it under our imprint.

Once authors are on our list, we assist them with the process of editing, handling the complexities of copyright, ISBN, Library of Congress card numbers, bar codes, as well as seeing that the published work is available on amazon.com and through international distributors like Ingram.

We also work with our authors to promote their books, helping them set up readings at local bookstores and libraries, putting them in touch with newspapers for reviews and radio stations for interviews, and publicizing their work on social media.

The Finger Lakes area is fertile with creative writers and we are proud to be in the forefront of helping them publish.

CLB is not, however, a regional imprint; we are happy to consider original poetry and prose by authors from all over the world on a wide variety of subjects.

Please see our website, www.cayugalakebooks.com for more information about us and a list of our books.

Made in the USA
Middletown, DE
10 September 2019